Praise for

THE BOOK OF MOODS

"Lauren Martin asks us to think much more, and much more deeply, about moods...In Martin's view, 'moody women' aren't bound to stigmas. They aren't irascible, irrational, or hormonal in a vacuum...Martin's message is relatable." —*Washington Post*

"In her engaging and informative new memoir, *The Book of Moods*, New York writer Lauren Martin tells of her personal journey from debilitating moodiness and anxiety to greater peace of mind...[*The Book of Moods*] feels like a conversation with a close friend." —*Psychology Today*

"[A] thoughtful take on how to prevent emotional responses from becoming negative moods." —*Publishers Weekly*

"Hilariously witty, unflinchingly honest, and brimming with hope, *The Book of Moods* teaches that with authenticity and a little self-coaching, you can take ownership of your emotions—and your own life. Lauren Martin's contagious curiosity leads straight to what she calls 'the cornerstone of chill.' And you know what? The journey is half the fun."

—Bobbi Brown, bestselling author and renowned makeup artist

"Lauren Martin names those feelings that we all have, explains why we have them, and how we can keep them from defining and dictating our lives. A fascinating, thorough, and truly helpful book. I loved it!"

—Sarah Knight, *New York Times* bestselling author of *Calm the F*ck Down*

"A deeply relatable how-to guide for managing your moods from a woman who gets it. This is a funny, moving memoir filled with so many a-ha moments that I had a hard time putting it down. A real asset for anyone on the quest for better emotion regulation and inner peace."

—Laurie Santos, professor of psychology at Yale University and host of *The Happiness Lab* podcast

"As someone who has struggled with understanding my own anxieties and stress surrounding social interactions, this book was a perfect read...I would highly recommend this book if you want to know more about communicating your feelings better and maintaining long-lasting, clear communication." —*Book Riot*

"Lauren's search for peace and well-being will help you navigate your very full plate." —*Good Morning America*

"In a memoir that is transparent and authentic, Martin walks us through all of the moods...Martin's prose also embraces and celebrates womanhood, just when we need it most." —*Shondaland*

"In addition to sharing her own struggles with anxiety, angst, and self-doubt, Martin calls upon clinical studies and stories from inspiring women (i.e., Audrey Hepburn, Princess Diana) to offer readers tangible tools for navigating their own whirlwind of emotions. Think of her book as a series of tried-and-true tactics for practicing self-care and emotional stability."

—*Shape* magazine

"Martin blends science, philosophy, witty anecdotes, and effective forms of self-care to show readers that you can turn your worst moods into your best life."
—*PureWow*

"Words of Women founder Lauren Martin delves into the relationship women have with negativity in her smart and often funny self-help tome, *The Book of Moods*. Martin explores her own struggles with anxiety and feelings of inferiority, alongside the science behind moods, to offer practical advice on how to practice effective self-care when negativity starts creeping in." —*PopSugar*

"Need a little therapy without an actual session? Many of us lead 'perfect' lives on the outside while speaking unspoken battles within us. Lauren Martin has a way of illuminating the science behind how we feel with intense clarity that will really help you feel more clear about things."
—*Glitter Guide*

"I think we'd all benefit from a book to help us with our emotions. Lauren Martin was more than happy to write a book for us...She uses her story to help readers understand their own. This book is proof you can give yourself the best life, despite those pesky negative moods."
—*The Tempest*

THE
BOOK
OF
MOODS

How I Turned My Worst
Emotions Into My Best Life

LAUREN MARTIN

FOUNDER OF WORDS OF WOMEN

GRAND CENTRAL
PUBLISHING

NEW YORK   BOSTON

Grand Central Publishing
Hachette Book Group
1290 Avenue of the Americas, New York, NY 10104
grandcentralpublishing.com
twitter.com/grandcentralpub

Originally published in hardcover and ebook in December 2020
First trade paperback edition: August 2022

Grand Central Publishing is a division of Hachette Book Group, Inc. The Grand Central Publishing name and logo is a trademark of Hachette Book Group, Inc.

The publisher is not responsible for websites (or their content) that are not owned by the publisher.

The Hachette Speakers Bureau provides a wide range of authors for speaking events. To find out more, go to www.hachettespeakersbureau.com or call (866) 376-6591.

Print book interior design by Sean Ford

Library of Congress Cataloging-in-Publication Data

Names: Martin, Lauren (Founder of Words of Women), author.
Title: The book of moods : how I turned my worst emotions into my best life
    / Lauren Martin, Founder of Words of Women.
Description: First edition. | New York, NY : Grand Central Publishing,
    [2020]
Identifiers: LCCN 2020022705 | ISBN 9781538733622 (hardcover) | ISBN
    9781538733615 (ebook)
Subjects: LCSH: Mood (Psychology) | Emotions. | Self-acceptance in women.
Classification: LCC BF521 .M37 2020 | DDC 152.4--dc23
LC record available at https://lccn.loc.gov/2020022705

ISBNs: 9781538733608 (trade paperback), 9781538733615 (ebook)

Printed in Canada

FRI

10 9 8 7 6 5 4 3 2 1

For Jay,
who has loved me, moods and all.

Although altogether too much of life is mood.

—Renata Adler, *Speedboat*

CONTENTS

THE MOOD: THE BODY

THE MOOD: UNFORESEEN CIRCUMSTANCES

THINGS THAT (*USED TO) PUT ME IN A MOOD:

A comment from my mother
Loud trucks
A bad photo
Strangers telling me I look like Claire Danes
Missed trains
Delayed planes
Long days at the office
Aggressive emails
Instagram stories
My face
My hair
My weight
Loud groups in small restaurants
Unreturned text messages

DISCLAIMER

This book is a collection of every bad mood I've ever had. Every fight, every breakdown, every moment lost. A map of every place I lost control because of some insignificant bump—a look, a comment, a thought. A list of every night I wasted in stress, in tears, in hate, in judgment, and every morning I squandered—missing the sunrise, the smell of the coffee, the warmth of my husband, the simple blessing of waking up—because something didn't *feel* right. It's a collection of all those moments, all those emotions, all the tiny, insignificant triggers that pushed me into them, and what I learned from it all.

After five years, a finished book, and hundreds (*thousands?*) of bottles of wine, I am still a moody woman. A woman who feels things deeply—the sting of a remark, the bite of a bad day, the pain of an unflattering photo. I am still passionate and sensitive and, at times, fragile. I still want to turn back some days, scream into the void, and smash the life I've constructed in a fit of anger. The difference now is that I am no longer controlled by these urges, these feelings, these thoughts. I am no longer a woman ruled by her moods.

I am no longer a woman who walks through the door ready to burst. A woman who assumes the moods of others, absorbing them and passing them off as her own. A woman who reacts and retaliates and rewinds scenarios like worn-out cassette tapes. No. None of that anymore. Now I expel. I radiate. I pass through. I know what my moods are—what provokes them, irritates them, and assuages them—and because I know what they are, I know how to transform them. Into love. Into compassion. Into good moods that collect and gather and make up a good life.

Five years ago, when I was younger and blonder and on track with the idea I had in my mind of where and how things should be, life was not good. It didn't get good, and I mean really good, until about six months ago, when this book was almost finished and I was sitting in my bedroom in my apartment in Brooklyn and realized I hadn't fought with my husband in over a year. I mean really fought, the way we used to, when I felt attacked and would say something so unnecessary, so wounding, I was surprised he never left me. And when I realized I no longer spent hours fretting over an unreturned text message or a cyst on my chin. When I went home for my twenty-ninth birthday and didn't spend the Amtrak ride back obsessing over a comment my mother made. It took a while because I had to go through each mood, find out what it was telling me, and practice on it, again and again, but I finally did it. And as I sit here now, reveling in the newfound comfort of knowing myself and the feelings that pulse through me, I can't stop thinking about how I would never have gotten here if it hadn't been for a stranger in a bar.

* * *

We met by chance on a cold, wet night in the middle of January. I was twenty-four, had just moved in with my boyfriend (now husband), and was miserable. Not sad. Not depressed. Just full of a white-hot agitation. There was something stirring at the bottom of my soul. Something had latched on and wouldn't get off.

I couldn't go back to the apartment this way. Not after last week, when I'd felt the same heaviness, arrived home under the same cloud, and yelled at Jay over the dishwasher. "You unpack it so aggressively," I said. We'd only moved in together three months earlier and I was already sabotaging it. *What's wrong with me? Why can't I just be happy?* These were the questions that plagued me as I walked up from the fluorescent underground of the subway onto the dark streets of Brooklyn. I needed to find something to soothe me, to knock off whatever had clamped itself to me. The only solution I could think of was alcohol, and the only bar I knew was five blocks past our apartment. Walking past my building, head down against the cold and the possibility of running into Jay or the doorman, I opened the heavy metal door with the neon sign above it, and that's when I saw her.

She had auburn hair, short and curled. She wore a mauve skirt and black pumps and was sitting alone nursing a martini. She wasn't beautiful in a traditional New York, supermodel way. I don't even remember what her face looked like. All I remember is that I couldn't stop wanting to catch a glimpse of her. She had what people describe as "an aura." She was one of those women you pass on the street and momentarily transplant your consciousness to and imagine going home to their world. Their beautiful house. Their handsome husband. Their perfect life. *I bet she never feels like this*, I thought. *I bet she goes home to her boyfriend and lovingly asks how his day was, gliding through the apartment, unfazed by the work emails pinging on her phone. I bet she lets things go with ease. Comments, texts, thoughts rolling off her like drops of water.*

She was only a few stools down from me, and when I brought out my book to pretend to read, I heard her say something. Assuming it was meant for someone else, I ignored it. But there was no reply, and when I looked up, she was staring at me. The radiant girl. "I love that author," she said again, smiling. So I scooted over one stool and she did too and now we were one stool away from each other, talking. Her name was Joanne and she was VP of sales at a large technology company in Manhattan. I don't remember much else she said about herself because I was too distracted studying her. She was confident and funny, sometimes loud during the punch line of a story, but absolutely charming. And that charm made her magnetic. And that magnetism created a different kind of elegance. Like a vessel of contained sunlight. All of these particles buzzing in perfect harmony.

After two drinks, we'd moved on to the more personal stuff. Like where I'd met my boyfriend. What my favorite book was. And why I was drinking two double whiskeys on a Monday night alone in a bar. She told me she was treating herself to a celebratory cocktail after closing a client. I took another sip and told her I was avoiding going home. That I just wasn't feeling like myself. I told her it was too difficult to explain. When she asked me to "just try," I couldn't hold it in anymore. Maybe I could try to explain it to myself. So I told her how the past few years I'd gotten everything I wanted—an apartment, a partner, a career in New York—yet I couldn't stay happy about it. How no matter how hard I tried, I kept breaking down, lashing out, ruining things. How it felt like the older I got, the less control I had over myself. How I was angry even when there was nothing to be angry about. Stressed even when I didn't need to be stressed.

Annoyed, irritable, and tense even though life was good. And I had no idea why.

When I'd finished, my drink untouched, hers half-gone, she was just sitting there, looking at me. My mind began to race. Did she think I was crazy? Had I shared too much? Was I scaring her?

"You feel it too," she finally said.

"Feel what?" I asked.

"These moods."

Is that what these were? These feelings I couldn't shake? These moments of tension, sensitivity, and despair? She didn't tell me I was stressed. Didn't tell me I needed a new boyfriend or a new job. She didn't tell me I was crazy. She had what I had. She felt it too. There's light in the words *I feel the same way.* There's sanity in a diagnosis. Together, those two things altered something in me, tightened a screw that stopped the shaking. *I have moods.* It was declaration more than hypothesis. I didn't care if what she said was right or wrong. Didn't care if she was crazy, if I'd just happened to catch her on a good day. It wasn't about her. It was about what she represented. Hope. Possibility. Change. There was something to measure. Something to observe, alter, and control. Walking out of the bar, dizzy from the whiskey and the revelation, I decided, then and there, that I would dedicate myself to figuring out these moods that ran through me.

WHAT ARE MOODS?

It is as if my life were magically run by two
electric currents: joyous positive and despair-
ing negative—whichever is running at the
moment dominates my life, floods it.

—Sylvia Plath

It's the small, unassuming comments people make that change us.
In fifth grade, Marla Cohen noted that I had "weird eyebrows."
This observation, made on a cafeteria bench beneath painted
letters of the alphabet, shifted some angle in my existence so
that for the rest of my life I will never be able to meet someone
without observing their eyebrows. I will never be able to watch
TV without noting the shape, the arch, the width of the actors'.
I will never be able to look in the mirror without thinking
about my own. Eyebrows are forever on my radar. Eyebrows, and
now moods.

Joanne's remark in that bar, which to anyone else would seem
so benign, so passing, unlocked an unconscious part of myself I'd
never understood or paid attention to, but now, like eyebrows, I
couldn't stop seeing. Is that why my sister was acting so stressed
and bitchy? Is she just in a mood? If so, does she know it? When
will she be out of it? When I talked to my boss on the phone
and she sounded different, tense, short, I wondered if she was in

a mood. When the Starbucks barista's disposition changed from friendly to terse between one latte and the next, I wondered if it wasn't because I was a bad tipper, but if, like everyone else, he was just in a mood.

I'd always been highly attuned to the energy of the people and places around me, always felt the subtle shift in affect the same way I felt the slightest drop in temperature. Now, as if overnight, my understanding of myself in relation to the world changed. It was lighter. Easier. Like finally learning the words to a song I'd been singing wrong for years. It all made sense. Knowing that other people's moods were just as random and uncontrollable as mine lightened the load of my interactions. For the first time, I realized their moods might have nothing to do with me.

That didn't mean I didn't still feel them. The more I paid attention to them, the more I saw how potent they were. How they leaked from one person to the next. How they hung in the air. How the slightest change in one person's mood altered another's. I watched how they leaked out of me, poisoning those near me. How my fumes wrapped around Jay's neck, slid up his nose, and pulled him under with me. How his mood would then snake along and infect his mother on the phone. *This is how it happens*, I thought. *How the world infects itself. One bad mood at a time.*

On the other side, I saw the charm and effect my good moods had. How when I was on form people opened up to me. How others gravitated to me the same way I had gravitated toward Joanne in the bar. How I could bring light and energy into a room, igniting it with my own spark. How the good moods danced and spun and transformed not just me but all those around me. How Jay fell in love with me, over and over again, when I was in a good mood. My good moods, I knew, were my best self.

And when I was my best self, I was on track. I was doing things that were good for me and good for those around me. I was able to go to the gym, eat healthy, listen intently, be kind. But when I was in a bad mood, all of my worst sides came out. I was sullen and mean and quick with a jab. I was disconnected and withdrawn or overly heightened. I brought the opposite of light, shrouding the space around me in misery. I overreacted, acted out of impulse, misread everything, alienated those I loved, and always woke up with the nauseating question *Why did I do that?*

Yet try as I might, I still didn't understand what the bad moods were. Still didn't know how to describe what was happening when I didn't feel like doing something, going somewhere, or being some way because I was *in a mood*. Still didn't know what was happening when the good mood was gone and the heaviness was back. They weren't just emotions. They were wider and denser and more complicated than feelings like sadness or anger. They felt like something in between, like the aftereffects of emotions. The charge that stayed in the air after a bomb.

Neuroscientists have confirmed that emotional responses last for only sixty to ninety seconds, so a mood, technically, is anything you feel after those ninety seconds. In *My Stroke of Insight: A Brain Scientist's Personal Journey*, neuroanatomist Dr. Jill Bolte Taylor wrote, "Once triggered, the chemical released by my brain surges through my body and I have a physiological experience. Within 90 seconds from the initial trigger, the chemical component of my anger has completely dissipated from my blood and my automatic response is over. If, however, I remain angry after those 90 seconds have passed, then it is because I have *chosen* to let that circuit continue to run." Buddhist monk Pema Chödrön also believes an emotion that lasts longer than a minute and a half is no longer an automatic response, but a decision to keep igniting that thought, that emotion, over and over again. According to Chödrön, if you allow an emotion to exist for ninety seconds without judging, it will disappear. Like with all self-help advice, the scientists and Buddhists made it seem so simple: *Let the emotion go and you won't have the mood. Stop feeling the thing and move on.* But it was so much more complicated than that. So much harder than that. I felt like the emotions came from nowhere, and before I realized what I was feeling, it was too late, I was already in a mood.

I also didn't understand why Jay didn't feel them as often or as deeply as I did, and the longer we lived together, the more I believed moods were more a woman's game. You could say women are predisposed to them. When brain scans were performed on men and women, a certain area of the brain lit up only in women when all participants were asked to clear their minds. This area of the brain, known as the paralimbic cortex, is used to filter emotional reactions to the environment, suggesting that even when women are at rest, their brains are registering and trying to process different emotional clues around them. Some researchers believe this is the reason for women's intuition. That we never actually stop taking in our environment. That we are never actually at rest.

Then there's the fact that women's brain function evolved differently from men's in response to maternal needs. Our ability to attach emotionally, to sense emotionality in others, has helped us keep our children safe and propagate the species, while making us more prone to depression and anxiety. Neuroscientists have also confirmed that women retain stronger and more vivid memories than men, along with the ability to recall memories faster and with more intensity. This may be the reason women are twice as likely than men to experience depression and post-traumatic stress disorder.

I also started noticing moods in everything I read about women. Every quote, every story, every interview seemed to have this underlying theme of emotional turmoil. When Ingrid Bergman recalled, "I remember one day sitting at the pool and suddenly the tears were streaming down my cheeks...I had success. I had security. But it wasn't enough. I was exploding inside." I knew how she felt, because I felt the same. When I listened to Stevie Nicks sing, "But never have I been a blue calm sea / I have always been a storm," I realized moods were not some rare disease only I was afflicted with. Moods were part of being a woman.

I knew this not just from what women said but from what people said about them. Journalist Jean-Paul Enthoven described French film star Françoise Dorléac as "beautiful, young, gifted, easy to laugh with, [with] a halo of anxiety around her." F. Scott Fitzgerald wrote to his wife, "If I didn't love you so much your moods wouldn't affect me so deeply." Director William Frye described Bette Davis as, "like so many great artists, a bundle of contradictions. On the one hand she could be a moody and petulant bully, who carefully cultivated inflexible opinions and fostered great hates. On the other she was a sensitive woman who—provided you were one of the few people she really liked—cared deeply about your health and happiness."

This was when Words of Women started. I needed a place to put down all I was finding, all I was learning, all that was helping me. In my lowest moment of despair, I started a blog. A place, a timeline, a holding space to keep track of all the words that were helping me. At least, that's what I told myself, but I think I also wanted company. Because one of the biggest moods that had been plaguing me was loneliness. Perhaps insecurity disguised as loneliness. Not loneliness by default but loneliness deep down by choice. Whatever the true motive, I needed to share what I was finding. Because I knew how I'd felt when I met Joanne, when I realized I was not alone, when someone said *I feel the same way*.

I only looked for women because I knew only women felt this. As Willa Cather said, "Only a Woman, divine, could know all that a woman can suffer." For the first time I felt understood. These women, these brilliant, artistic, successful women felt the same way I did. Which is why I ended up calling the blog Words of Women. (It's also why most quotes in this book are by women.)

I didn't just share a quote or an interview, but the story behind each woman. Because the story was what made the quote interesting. The story was what made it resonate. And then I started sharing how the quote helped me, how it filled the empty spaces, softened the ridges of loneliness and fear. When I started doing that, sharing my most intimate feelings, I knew I was onto something bigger than my own journey. I was helping other women understand their own feelings. I was interrupting their Instagram feed of models and airbrushed ads with something real, something that spoke to the challenges we were all facing. I was sending emails that weren't filled with cookie recipes and advice for better skin care but were about my bad day, the anxiety I felt writing, and the quotes that were helping me through it.

The more I read, saw, and heard about women, the more I understood that moods were a power as much as a curse. Good moods created a radiance, a magnetism, an aura that attracted people with the same strength and propensity that the bad moods repelled. They were two sides of the same coin. To get rid of my moods would mean to get rid of both the light and the dark, leaving me with nothing but white space, like one of those empty-shell women you meet who have no glow, no life, no spark to them. I didn't want to get rid of my moods, I realized. I wanted to harness them.

WHERE DO MOODS COME FROM?

> I'm so sorry for all the times I've been mean and hateful—for all the miserable minutes I've caused you when we could have been so happy.
>
> —Zelda Fitzgerald, from a letter to
> F. Scott Fitzgerald

My good moods didn't seem to come from anywhere. They felt like my natural state. When I was happy, I was myself. When I was in a bad mood, I was someone else. Good moods always felt the same, whereas bad moods always felt different—had different tastes, weights, degrees. There was the mood I felt when I passed an Instagram story of friends hanging out without me. That subtle shift, the change in me that lingered over something as innocent as a photo. Then there was the mood I felt when my aunt made a remark about my weight at Christmas. The words locking on to my soul and weighing me down in a different way.

And then there was the mood at work, the one that bubbled up in the middle of the afternoon when I was tired of staring at my computer, when the thought of taking the crowded subway home created a restlessness I couldn't shake. In recording all these moods, I noticed a pattern. These feelings, these bad moods, were always triggered by some *thing*. A photo. A thought. A comment. If my good moods were my natural state, then my bad moods were when something brought me out of it.

I'd always been told to watch out for the big things in life. Death. Disease. Poverty. Those were the things that could hurt me. Those were the things that brought misery and suffering. Those were the things that could ruin my life. No one ever told me about all the small things. The plane delays, the subway commute, the adult acne. The aggressive emails and rude comments. The photos, the wrong angle in the mirror, the thoughts of yesterday and tomorrow. All the tiny things that nicked and scratched me daily, my wounds never healing, scabs never forming. After all these years I started to understand it. **It wasn't about my moods. It was about my triggers.**

My triggers were the unique set of things that had the power to push my buttons. If I could avoid my triggers, I could avoid the emotions that would follow. For a while, I tried to avoid all the things I knew triggered me. I got off social media. I called my mom less often. I changed jobs. I changed haircuts. But getting rid of one trigger only unveiled another one. The less I went on social media, the more beautiful girls I noticed at bars, in magazines, on billboards. The less I spoke with my mom, the more comments from Jay or my boss or some friend bothered me. The less I commuted, the more I ran into things at home I couldn't stand.

Triggers, I realized, couldn't be avoided. They were part of the experience of life. They were unchangeable, immutable, unavoidable. Psychologists define triggers as stimuli that prompt the recall of a traumatic memory. Mood experts, psychologists, and scientists have also defined moods as responses to feelings triggered by events. Even though whatever triggered the emotion is gone, the mood is still there. Moods weren't just about understanding my emotions, but the triggers that prompted them.

I finally understood that moods didn't come out of thin air. That the feelings that plagued me, the anxiety, the anger, the fear, the hurt, didn't come from some unknown place within, but from these small, mundane triggers outside. And the triggers weren't making me miserable, my reactions to them were.

I couldn't do anything about a delayed plane. A crowded subway. A pimple on my wedding day. **The only things I could control were my perceptions and reactions to the random, unpleasant circumstances.** Because I can't always stop what happens to me. The events of life are too unpredictable, indeterminable, and unchangeable. My triggers were lessons. Reminders. A buzzer that went off when I hit something in myself that needed attention. A sharp corner that would keep cutting me until I learned my way around it.

Unlike Elizabeth Gilbert or Cheryl Strayed, my journey did not take me to ashrams and through desert plains, but across an isolated span of time in New York City. Five years wandering throughout the dirty, mundane crevices of reality. The female experience. The small things that hurt me, poked me, and wounded me. The comments, the unreturned texts, the fights, the zits, the delays. The triggers of my life.

Throughout this book, I'll take you on my own personal voyage into the depths of my emotions, to uncover the hidden meaning and underlying truths behind each mood that kept me from living my best life. Each of the following chapters features a moment in time over the past five years. A moment when I caught myself mid-mood. When some event, some tiny, seemingly insignificant thing nicked me and I was able to notice it, record it, and understand it enough to identify it. Over the following days, weeks, months, I'd study it. Dissect it. Practice on it. Because even though that specific moment was gone, another one like it would come. I tried techniques to use the next time I felt a similar way, a similar mood, a similar trigger. I borrowed advice from doctors, psychologists, and hundreds of the women I'd read about. And the ones that stuck with me, the ones that I still use today, the ones that I know work, that can kick a mood out before it begins, are the ones I'm going to share with you.

Within the past five years I got married, lost friends, gained new ones, started a new job, moved apartments, and fought with my fiancé in the middle of Bloomingdale's. In these moments, however, I was unlike I'd ever been before—aware. Observing my pain while living it. Analyzing my responses while regretting them. Sliding into a mood while marking it. And in being aware of the moods that overtook me, the feelings that passed through me, I acquired something I never had before: distance. And with that distance, I was able to study myself.

Before, I had just fallen into moods. I would wake up to find myself drowning in the middle of them. Now I was standing beside myself, examining them. *Yes, I am feeling this*, I'd think. *But why? What's it trying to tell me?* By questioning what I once thought were natural reactions to natural feelings, I started to grasp the underlying issue. The deeper, more rooted problem. A problem that would continue to occur in various forms until it was fixed. And after so much time, so many moods, so much distance, I transformed from a sensitive, insecure, moody woman to a woman who can now conquer, move through, and accept the worst moments of life, transforming them into knowledge, power, and calm.

THE MOOD:

THE PAST AND FUTURE

Symptoms include: dissociation, running thoughts, and repeated usage of the phrase *I'm so stressed*.

THE MOOD DESCRIBED

It's like I got to wear blinders all the time so
I won't think sideways or in the past.
—Carson McCullers, *The Heart Is a
Lonely Hunter*

You remember too much,
my mother said to me recently.

Why hold onto all that? And I said,
Where can I put it down?
—Anne Carson, "The Glass Essay"

Looking back is a misery, I don't remember
what was fun and funny; I remember what I
wish to forget, the wrong sad hurting things.
—Martha Gellhorn

It was the Tuesday after Memorial Day. Jay and I had just gotten off the subway in Brooklyn, slightly tanned, pulling our suitcases behind us. The air was warm, a cool breeze carrying the last farewell of winter and the aroma of the flowers, now beginning to bloom, mixed with the dirt and sweat of New York, creating that undeniable scent. The smell of possibility. I'd just begun writing this book, and though I had no deal or agent or idea that it would someday be published, the future lay in front of me like a calm sea. I forgot that my mind, like the sea, could turn. That moods, like storms, rolled in even on the calmest of days.

On the way back to the apartment we'd decided to pick up some ingredients for dinner: milk, steak, and a tomato. Jay offered to go inside, fighting the crowds and maze of aisles, while I waited with the luggage. I remember standing there, the lower edge of my bum resting on the top edge of a fire hydrant, the two black suitcases next to me, thinking how lucky I was. Lucky to live in New York. Lucky to have a boyfriend who did things like run inside so I could stay outside. Lucky to be young, in love, and smelling the sweet air.

Then my phone vibrated. I pulled it from my back pocket, swiping on an email notification. I was working for a marketing agency, and even though it was a holiday weekend, my boss wanted to know when I'd have next week's presentation ready. The message was no more than ten words. Just one line. Yet the aggressive tone, less asking and more demanding, flipped a switch. Some small lever inside me set in motion a projector of thoughts, playing in quick succession like a silent film. I thought about how I didn't want to go to work tomorrow. How everything—the commute, the emails, the meetings—would drain whatever peace I'd found during the weekend. I thought about the last presentation I'd given. The way my hands started to sweat and the way the client had that glazed-over look in their eyes. I thought about when Becky, my coworker, had pointed out the spelling mistake in my copy options. Becky was such a bitch. Or maybe she wasn't. Maybe those spelling errors were why no literary agents were calling me back. Maybe this book was a bad idea.

Jay's reappearance startled me, rattling me out of my trance. For fifteen minutes I'd been trying to stand with good posture, trying to exude an aura of carefreeness, angled to my good side so he would walk out and remember why he fell in love with me. But in the midst of all my thoughts, I forgot about my plan, and when he appeared from the slid- ing exit doors, I was contorted, hunched over, my face in a snarl.

"Thanks for waiting, Mother Teresa," he joked.

"Uh, yeah. Sure. Was it crowded?" I couldn't help my tone. It was flat, like reading off a script for a play I didn't want to be in.

"Yeah, Jesus Christ. Like, is Whole Foods the cool place to hang now?" He was trying to make me laugh.

"I guess so." I drew my breath but instead of pausing, exhaled into another sentence. "Can we just get home already? I have a million things to do."

I could tell from the forlorn look on his face that I was catching him off guard, ripping him from the same trance I'd ripped myself from. "Jeez," he said. "What crawled up your ass?"

"I just want to get home," I said, exasperated, exuding the opposite image of the one I wanted to portray. But I couldn't stop myself. I couldn't change course.

"Good thing we're almost there," he said, speaking not to me but straight ahead at the five blocks in front of us, at the end of which our apartment sat. I knew what he was thinking. What the hell had happened? How had he walked through the door and come out the other side to a different woman? How had I gone from calm to stressed in under fifteen minutes? Nothing had happened, nothing besides a simple email anyway, yet everything was different.

WHAT THE MOOD IS TELLING YOU

I didn't know what had happened either. Two minutes earlier things were great. Spring had arrived like a cool glass of water and I had been grateful to be coming home to my apartment with the newly blossomed trees. Grateful to be in love. Grateful to be in New York. Grateful to have what I'd wanted for so long. Then, suddenly, everything was dark. The sweetness in the air was gone, the love I felt for Jay had dissipated, and the open horizon of dreams and possibilities felt like a vast desert I would never cross. Life felt hard and unfair and tight around my neck.

By the time we got back to the apartment, I told Jay I was too exhausted to start cooking right away. Instead, I splayed myself on the couch, reflexively put on Netflix, and looked for something to distract me from the tidal wave of thoughts creating a pool of anger and resentment. It was too late. My calm spell from the three-day weekend had broken and I was in a tailspin. Everything I thought triggered some other thought about some *thing* I had to do.

All the Things I Have to Do

- Have the perfect wedding—because people are driving and flying down for this.
- Reproduce—but don't get pregnant right away.
- Be successful—but at a job that can handle you leaving when you do get pregnant.
- Be healthy—but don't waste too much money on organic groceries.
- Be beautiful—but don't spend all your salary trying.
- Stop drinking alcohol—but also be more social.
- Respond to those emails from work—and stop letting your inbox get so full.
- Save money—or just stop spending money.
- Pay the rent—which I pay too much for.
- Pick up my prescriptions—and delete all the voice mails from Walgreens.
- Buy a house—which is a pipe dream based on the amount I'm spending every month on rent.

The thoughts poured in one atop the other, the tension inside me mounting as I racked my brain for someone to blame—like

I was trying to attribute every thought, every painful memory, every future problem to some person, some reason. I wouldn't be stressed about getting pregnant if my mom hadn't made those comments. I wouldn't be worried about being beautiful if society didn't make me feel this way. I wouldn't have to pay so much in rent if Jay hadn't picked such an expensive neighborhood. But all my arguments had holes. All my blame was misdirected. This was life, and none of it was anyone's fault. When I'd exhausted all my deluded projections, I was left with nothing but myself and the realization that this was just my *I'm so stressed about everything* mood.

I'd seen my mom get in this mood—usually when we were getting ready to go on a trip. She'd start obsessing over how messy the house was and how much work she still had to do, and how we were going to hit traffic on the way to the airport, which would mean we could miss our flight. We'd grown accustomed to ignoring her in this state, turning inward and steering clear when her voice grew stiff and affected. We didn't dare offer help, for years past had taught us she didn't actually need it and whatever task we'd do would lead to something else that was wrong or never right.

Instead, we'd clench our backpacks or the car's door handles and watch the blood roll from our father's neck to his face, until he'd finally let out a scream asking her to chill out. But she couldn't or wouldn't, and now one stiff parent was two, and lying on the couch in my Brooklyn apartment, with Jay unpacking the groceries, I had that aching realization, the same one I had when I shouted and the voice that came out was strange yet all too familiar—I was turning into my mother.

Unlike my mother, I found that my mood affected me at the

end of trips, rather than the beginning. While she couldn't shut off without sputtering, I couldn't turn back on without jolting. Either way, we couldn't adjust. We couldn't move from state to state, event to event, moment to moment without tensing and reacting. It was like we kept getting caught in our own way, tripping and choking on our own thoughts. Only later did I learn this mood was anxiety.

Anxiety is defined by the American Psychological Association as "an emotion characterized by feelings of tension, worried thoughts and physical changes." Feelings about things that *could* happen. Things that *will* happen. "It's funny," Simone de Beauvoir said once, "how she's scared of things in advance—quite frantically so." Research shows that women worry twice as much as men, making us twice as likely to suffer from anxiety. Women are also more likely to make connections between bad events in the past and possible negative events in the future, a cognitive bias known as anchoring. There's a story about Barbra Streisand that perfectly explains this phenomenon.

In 1967 Streisand was at the height of her fame. She'd just finished filming *Funny Girl* and was touring for her new album. At a concert in Central Park she forgot the words to a song, freezing in front of 150,000 people. Whether anyone noticed or not, the concert continued, and Streisand went on to receive fifty-two Gold, thirty-one Platinum, and thirteen Multi-Platinum Awards, making her the only woman to make the All Time Top 10 Best Selling Artist list.

But none of that mattered. She was so humiliated, so upset, so jarred by her Central Park experience that she refused to tour again for nearly thirty years. She told Diane Sawyer, "I didn't sing and charge people for twenty-seven years because of that night...I was like, 'God, I don't know. What if I forget the words again?'"

In 1994 she announced plans to take the stage again and her tickets sold out overnight, with Streisand garnering as much as $10 million per evening. To this day, however, she says that the anxiety of the Central Park concert will keep her from touring unless she really wants something—like the Modigliani painting she wanted badly enough to agree to a Netflix special. "I can't work for money. I have to work for an object that I love."

Streisand, like so many of us, is boxed in by her fear. It's as if she got a glimpse of the bad way her performance could have gone and was so scared of it happening that she decided to avoid it for the rest of her life. This attachment to the past, this anxiety that arises due to fear, is the plague of womanhood. It's the past and the future pushing against us, removing us from not just reality but our own clarity. We can't function in this state. We miss out on our lives in this state. When we're anxious, we're not really living. We're surviving. We're holding on, waiting for the anxiety to pass, losing out on minutes, hours, and days of our lives.

The answer was so clear, so obvious. Stop thinking about the future and fretting over the past. Anxiety was nothing more than thinking. Rapid, untrained thinking. But even if I took years off to attend workshops, silent retreats, and meditation circles, I knew I'd never be able to truly stop my thoughts. My mind would always find a way to wander to dark memories of the past and spend minutes in lines, waiting rooms, and sleepless nights projecting into the future.

The past was too heavy and the future too forceful to truly escape. Instead, I'd have to learn to travel through the recesses of my mind, back and forth between the three plateaus—past, present, future—with the confidence of a sailor, riding the waves as they came.

REMEMBER THE WRITERS

> I do believe...that everything you need to know about life can be learned from a genuine and ongoing attempt to write.
>
> —Dani Shapiro, *Still Writing*

To study this mood, I didn't need to seek out experiences that made me anxious. I didn't need to hope something would happen. I didn't need to look out for the moments to practice on. I was in the middle of the most anxious period of my life.

Writing a book, I quickly found out, was a crash course in anxiety. Years of being locked in a room with nothing but my thoughts, my future, my past in front of me. At the start of the dream, I hadn't thought about the pain that would accompany it, only the excitement. Three months in, however, I was in the middle of the ocean, wailing and sputtering, drowning myself in fear. Never had I experienced such intense moments of frustration, pain, and anxiety over white space, blank pages, empty inboxes. I was crying in the shower, my right eye was twitching, and I'd picked up a new habit of chewing my hair. *I can't do it*, I thought. *There's too much I don't know, too much I can't see.* I felt like Joan Didion when she described writing *Slouching Towards Bethlehem*:

"The pain kept me awake at night and so for twenty and twenty-one hours a day I drank gin-and-hot-water to blunt the pain and took Dexedrine to blunt the gin and wrote the piece."

Only I wasn't writing the piece. I was sitting there for hours on end with nothing to show for it.

Every time I sat down to write, the anxiety enveloped me. *What if no one buys it? What if I don't finish? What if I'm not allowed to write again?* I'd spend three hours in front of the page without a word, leaving the bedroom only to pour myself whiskey. The future of the book and my past writing failures, those juvenile stories in college, those terrible articles on the internet, tumbled and crashed against me. It was the same paralysis, the same self-questioning, that kept me awake at night. The same fear and doubt that kept me tossing and turning while Jay slept soundly beside me. I couldn't write in this state. I could barely function in this state.

I needed to find something to ground me. Something to help me out of my own head. So while I poured whiskey with one hand, I researched with the other. I went back to what I always did, tried to see how other women handled it. I filled journals with quotes from writers, artists, leaders. I watched interviews with Pulitzer Prize–winning authors and Nobel laureates. I read the *Paris Review* and the *New Yorker*, combing articles for advice, inspiration, an answer to how these women kept themselves afloat in the sea of the unknown. How they kept themselves grounded in the face of all that was ahead.

Writing advice, I found out, was just life advice. The same way writers tackled the blank page was how I should tackle life.

Writers on Tackling Anxiety

Build a corner. This is what people who are good at puzzles do. They ignore the heap of colors and shapes and simply look for straight edges. They focus on piecing together one tiny corner.

—Dani Shapiro, *Still Writing*

To make something good of the future, you have to look the present in the face.

—Simone de Beauvoir, *The Mandarins*

When I sit down to work, I'm just trying to get one little thing right.

—Deborah Eisenberg

Forget about the wide world and all that anxiety and just do it, one word after the other.

—Anne Enright

Remember who you are and where you are and what you're doing.

—Katherine Anne Porter

The consensus was obvious: Stay present. Stay with what's in front of you. Don't get ahead of yourself, don't worry about the middle and the ending, just stick with the page you're on. Of all the writers, the hundreds of Sylvia Plath and Patti Smith and Agatha Christie quotes, Jane Smiley, author of fourteen books and the recipient of the Pulitzer Prize for fiction, explained it most clearly. "Writing," she said, "is only one word at a time. It's not a whole bunch of things happening at once. Various things can present themselves, but when you face the page, it's a couple of words, and then a couple more words, and, if you're lucky, a sentence or a paragraph."

It was so simple yet so profound. So obvious yet so overlooked. One word at a time. One sentence. One book. It mimicked the structure of life. One moment. One day. One life. As books were written in words, life was lived in moments. The word I was paying attention to would lead to the next. The moment I was living in now would roll into my future.

When I went back to write, I noticed that when I focused on the words in front of me, the fears about the rest of the book dissolved. The same thing happened when I focused on the moment. Actually, when I focused on the moment, two things happened: I didn't have the time or mental space to worry about the future, and because I was paying attention to the moment, the future took care of itself. Because the future was the result of moments, and when I was living as presently in the moment as possible, I didn't have to worry so much about *what could be*. When I took care of the dishwasher now, I didn't have to find time to do it later. When I did well on my work presentation, I didn't need to worry about the security of my job, the scrutiny of my boss, later. When I focused on this chapter, I didn't need to fear the one after it. And that's when I began trusting myself, in a way I never had before. I trusted myself to live in the present, in a way that would take care of my future self. And the more I trusted myself, the less I saw myself worrying about the future.

SWIPE LEFT

> Anything I cannot transform into something
> marvelous, I let go.
>
> —Anaïs Nin

Just paying attention to when I left the present was a vital step in overcoming this mood. The way an addict has to watch for cravings, I had to watch my wandering mind, notice when it was happening so I didn't follow it, unconsciously, down the dark path it led. But it was hard to notice something I wasn't used to noticing. How could I notice something my brain automatically does?

Our mind wanders during 47 percent of our waking hours, with brain activity in the frontal lobe sparking up every time we try to rest. Our memory, cognition, and learning are all housed in the part of the brain that jumps into gear when we try to turn off. Known as the default mode network, it's why when you walk to the subway your brain automatically starts to recall the past, or why when you're taking a shower you remember what you forgot at the grocery store. And it's confirmed that at least one-third of the brain's thoughts come out negative. In fact, research found that people are happier doing unpleasant tasks, like sitting in traffic or waiting in lines, than not doing anything and letting their minds wander.

But if the brain can wander off, it can also be pulled back in. According to MRI scans, it takes twelve seconds to redirect our attention once we've noticed our mind has wandered. Those who meditate can redirect it even quicker. Due to the neuro-plasticity of the brain, when we practice certain actions, they become habits, and over time, the brain rewires itself according to those habits and their cues. If you've been practicing the art of meditation for years, your brain is highly alert to when the mind starts wandering and that much quicker at bringing it back to the present.

I hated that fact, though. I was tired of hearing about it. *Meditation is linked to less stress. Meditation is linked to better health.* I hated how the answer to good health was based on something I'd never be able to do. Like cartwheels and French braids, I just couldn't wrap my mind around this thing that was supposed to be so simple. I bought candles, downloaded apps, and spent several hours perusing spiritual bookshops. But every time I tried to sit in bed and breathe, it felt wrong. This wasn't me. I couldn't do it. I'd just gotten myself to start flossing.

Instead, I turned back to my writers, and a few weeks later Dani Shapiro answered it for me. In her book *Still Writing*, she compares writing to meditating, quoting Sharon Salzberg and her suggestion that "the real skill, in meditation, is simply noticing that the mind has wandered."

That one sentence unlocked a new understanding of medita-tion. The concept was something practical and tactical I could apply. I didn't need the right app to do that. I didn't need to spend ten minutes alone in my bedroom every morning. I just needed to take notice. Instead of being angry at myself when my mind wandered, I could use it as a cue.

I learned that a good way to practice noticing my thoughts was to practice noticing everything else. I learned this from a piece of writing advice I'd heard somewhere long ago: *For every different room in which you find yourself on every single day, point out at least one thing that is there, but shouldn't be there, and why it shouldn't be there.* This advice struck me because it was fun. It was engaging. It reminded me of all the ways I'd learned the other fundamental lessons of my life. ABCs through song. Spanish words through games. State capitals through mnemonic devices.

So that's what I did, I made my anxious thoughts into a game. I was on the lookout for any time my mind wandered, and like playing whack-a-mole, would jump on it and crush it. *Awful memory of that time I was in Punta Cana when I fell in the middle of the bar.* Whack. *Sudden anxious thought about the possibility of getting cancer and dying.* Whack. *Uncomfortable feeling that I will never get married or have kids and will spend my future alone.* Whack. I wasn't worried about stopping the thoughts or dealing with them, just intent on noticing them. In noticing them, however, I realized how ridiculous they were. How the future was none of my business and the past was no longer my problem. Instead of getting stuck in that memory, the anxious thought, I began to see it as just another thought to be whacked.

When I was talking to Jay about this one evening, he told me he did something similar, but with Tinder. "Since when are you on Tinder?" I asked, half joking.

Obviously, he said, it had been years, but the mechanism of it got caught in his brain, the concept of swiping left or right, and that's what he did now with his thoughts. "When I don't like something I'm thinking about, I just swipe." I liked how simple his interpretation of it was. Just like my piece of writing advice, but easier to grasp, to explain, to comprehend.

The more I practiced it, the easier it became, until eventually it turned into a habit. And just like any habit, the more I did it, the less I had to think about doing it. Of course, I sometimes forget. I still find myself sitting on the couch, zoned out, immersed in some nightmare memory only to come back to reality pissed off and worn out. But even when that happens there's a small shred of the game there. I lost that one, but I'll get the next one.

ACCEPT THE WORST

> The thing about life is that you must survive. Life is going to be difficult, and dreadful things will happen. What you do is move along, get on with it, and be tough.
>
> —Katharine Hepburn

When I did start to notice, when I became acutely aware of my wandering mind, I started to pay more attention to where it went. Daydreams were when it went somewhere pleasant. A mood was when it went somewhere dark. And the dark places were at the end of the maze of what-ifs my mind followed. *What if my wedding is awful? What if I embarrass myself? What if the plane is delayed? What if I get fired? What if I don't get the job at all?* All of these what-ifs are rooted in pain. The pain of rejection. The pain of discomfort. The pain of failure. It's this pain I feared. The pain of the worst what-if.

Women have an interesting relationship to pain. We're born expecting it, live in anticipation of it, accepting the blows, the cramps, the labor pains as they arise. Yet when it comes to pain outside of the body, pain in the form of betrayals, embarrassment, and losses, we fear it with childish trepidation.

In 1948 doctors wanted to create a pain measurement scale to understand how to appropriately gauge pain levels. The experiment was performed on pregnant women going into labor. Between contractions, a doctor would apply a heat gun to the woman's hand and ask her to compare the pain of the heat to the pain of her contractions. The doctor would increase the heat until the woman felt the pain matched the pain of her contractions. The pain scale, known as the dolorimeter, measured intensity of pain in dols, stopping at 10.5 dols when one woman received second-degree burns. The dolorimeter is still debated in the scientific community as an accurate measurement tool for pain, however, because even with the second-degree burns, the woman did not move her hand away. They could not measure the totality of the pain without inflicting physical injury. You could say the dolorimeter stops at 10.5, but a woman's pain goes much further.

I couldn't wrap my mind around it—how we cope with these horrible inevitabilities, these traumatic, painful experiences, yet the thought of a bad date or an overscheduled day sends us into panic. How do we go to war with beasts yet scream over mice? Maybe because we can't do anything about the pain we're destined to endure, we focus on the pain we think we can avoid.

Maybe the loss of control of our bodies is manifested in our need to control the world around us.

"Worry," Rebecca Solnit believes, "is a way to pretend that you have knowledge or control over what you don't." The degree to which this uncertainty bothers us is the degree of our anxiety. And the degree to which we try to control the uncertainty of our lives is the way so many of us waste our lives. All of those times that we spend the day, or the conversation, or the entire relationship stressing about things that never come to pass—those lost moments are the ones that we sacrifice at the altar of our fear of pain. We're so scared of pain that we inflict a different kind of pain trying to avoid it.

So, what if we just accepted the inevitability of pain and then kept going? Imagine if you accepted the pains of the unknown as unflinchingly as you accepted the pain of the known. This concept is the core tenet of Stoicism—a philosophy practiced in ancient Greece and Rome and considered the building blocks of Buddhism. The word *stoic* has many definitions, but its general connotation is "indifferent to pain." I've also heard it described as heroic acceptance. And that's how I like to think of it. A grit one has developed to accept whatever pain will come. It is strength of character and a unique sort of courage to live your daily life ready to deal with pain.

The philosophy is best explained in a story about the philosopher Seneca. Around AD 65 one of Seneca's friends wrote to him. He was in trouble, he claimed. He'd just found out about a lawsuit against him and he feared it would destroy his credibility or lead to prison or exile. He was, as any of us would be, in a state of panic. Seneca wrote back with advice: Accept exile. Accept rejection. Accept that you will be humiliated. Accept that the worst will happen. If you lose this case, can anything more severe happen to you than being sent into exile or prison? The point of his letter was not to calm his friend's worst thoughts, but to make him comfortable with them. "Hope for that which is utterly just, and prepare for that which is utterly unjust," he advised.

I wanted to be one of these stoic people, to see things rationally and calmly. Soon enough, I had the perfect opportunity to practice that train of thought when I made my first *real* mistake at work. It was a few weeks after I got the email from my boss outside Whole Foods. The presentation she was asking about, the one I spent the next week stressing over, went great and we'd signed the client. Everything was on track until I walked into the office a week later and found the newly printed flyers on my desk.

My job as account executive for a marketing company included handling the design assets for clients. This particular client was high profile, and doing something as small as designing their flyers for a music festival was a huge opportunity. After the payments had been made, the designs approved and then re-approved, the fonts changed, the wording moved, and the colors swapped, I was happy to have them done and almost out of my hands and into the clients'. I did a quick scan over the sample flyer on the top of the box, then called a courier to deliver them. There were at least ten thousand, so there would have to be a truck, not a cyclist, for this kind of delivery.

Two hours later my boss called me into her office. There was a frantic tone to her voice I hadn't heard before. "Did you approve the copy on the flyers?" she asked me. I hesitated before answering. Was this a trick question?

"Yes," I said.

"So you didn't notice it?"

"Notice what?" I asked, my blood pressure rising.

"That Denver is spelled 'Dover.' That ten thousand flyers were printed and shipped that say the festival is in *Dover, Colorado!*"

"Oh, shit." I meant to say it in my head, but I said it out loud.

"Oh shit is right," she said.

I left her office, head down, hurriedly walking past the rows of cubicles and inquiring coworkers to cry in the bathroom. Sitting on the toilet, surrounded by rolls of toilet paper and Lysol air fresheners, I thought about how dark everything was. How I would get fired. How the client would sue our company. How someone might find out about the account executive who printed the ten thousand flyers with the misspelled word and I'd become a black sheep of the industry. I'd never work again. But I was just one person! How was I supposed to catch everything? It had been a hectic month and on top of those flyers I had hundreds of other tasks for a handful of other clients. The excuses didn't make me feel better. I knew that this was just one of those adult mistakes I'd heard about but never truly experienced. One of those moments that had no bail-out button. No mom, boyfriend, loophole to save me. Then I remembered stoicism. This was my time to practice it. This was a situation that had a worst outcome in sight, and I could either accept it or fight against it.

So I accepted it. I did everything I could first, which included doing something I wasn't used to doing—accepting responsibility. Asking for both help and forgiveness. While emailing the flyer distributor to see if they'd give us a refund and making the difficult call to the client to explain the situation, I realized that half the pain of mistakes came from the aversion to owning up to them. We're so scared of admitting to fault, we'll do anything we can to avoid it, and in doing that we take the longer, harder road out. But as I watched myself apologize, without excuses, without shifting blame, I noticed how much easier it was to just lean into the mistake. Once I admitted it and accepted the responsibility for it, people were more apt to help me. Less time was wasted on trying to figure out who to blame (because I'd already volunteered) and more time was spent on how the crisis could be handled.

By the time I left for the weekend I'd done everything I could do—admitted, apologized, begged for mercy, then sat back and prepared for the worst. I accepted that I would be out of a job. I accepted that the client would fire us. I accepted that my career might be over. And when I accepted these fates, rather than denying them or trying to avoid them, my anxiety decreased. And then you know what happened? I woke up to an email from the flyer distributor saying they would give me a discount on the reprint. But I wouldn't need it, because two days later one of the interns had the idea of crossing out all the O's in *Dover* and writing *en* above them, which actually looked retro cool. The whole office pitched in and hand-corrected ten thousand flyers in black Sharpie in time for the event. Even though we lost the client after that, and I was out of favor with my boss for the next few months, it didn't bother me. Because once I'd accepted the bleakest situation, everything else felt like a blessing.

When you accept the inevitability of the pain and discomfort that the future holds, you can let go of the fear of uncertainty. These paralyzing whirlwinds of possibilities—how much pain, when the pain will happen, how bad the pain will be—are what create the tension within us. When we accept the worst possibility, all the other possibilities fall away and the tension is released.

SEE THE PAST AS A STORY

> Because if I tell the story, I can make you
> laugh, and I would rather have you laugh at
> me than feel sorry for me.
>   Because if I tell the story, it doesn't hurt
> as much.
>   Because if I tell the story, I can get on
> with it.
>
> —Nora Ephron, *Heartburn*

Over time, the future became easier to reconcile with. All it was, I realized, was an idea. An idea of how things could go. Like daydreams, the future was nothing more than a figment of my imagination, something I could change or mold at whim. The past, however, wasn't as malleable. The past was fixed, planted and rooted. It was a box I tried to keep shut and shoved in the corner. And I would have kept avoiding it, kept throwing my weight against it to keep it from busting open, if Nora Ephron hadn't taught me that there was no way I could be a writer, a friend, a success, if I didn't walk over to the box and dump the contents on the floor.

Nora Ephron's life was one I aspired to. Before I discovered her books, there were her movies: *When Harry Met Sally*, *You've Got Mail*, *Sleepless in Seattle*, *Julie & Julia*. This woman, I thought, had the perfect life, the perfect career, the perfect mind. It wasn't until living in New York, obsessing over my own writing failures and aspirations, that I found out if it hadn't been for her imperfect past, none of her books, then none of her movies, would ever have been made.

In 1979, just three years after getting married and moving to Washington, Ephron was pregnant with her second child when she found out her husband, Pulitzer Prize–winning journalist Carl Bernstein, was cheating on her with Margaret Jay, a woman, according to Nora, "with a neck as long as an arm and a nose as long as a thumb." That horrible moment, the moment she'd returned to New York and given birth to her child alone, was the darkest of her life. Four years later, it would become the brightest.

"What she did," explains director Mike Nichols, "is in mid-jump she moved to the Gottliebs' house and cried for six months and wrote it funny. And in writing it funny, she won. And be-trayed women all over the world knew it and cheered." Her book *Heartburn* was an account of the experience and became not just an international bestseller but a stepping-stone into her career as a novelist and filmmaker.

This idea of seeing the past as funny was nothing new to Nora, however. The daughter of writers, she was instructed to "take notes" throughout her life and any bad situation, any embarrass-ing moment, anything that was the worst thing of her life was only material for a great story.

When you enter the past, you're entering a zone of *that time*. People reported one-third of their memories as bad when asked to recall the past. The human condition is ingrained with regret and painful memories. When we're drawn back to the past, we're forced to remember things we wish we could forget. Like that time in high school I went to my friend Jimmy's swim club with his family and thought I'd look cool doing a swan dive off the board, only to be told by Jimmy that his family wanted me to know my bathing suit was see-through. Or that time I lied about my name in college and used a British accent. Or that time I said my SAT scores were a thousand points higher or said that stupid thing in that stupid class where I wore that stupid shirt. You know, that time that was the worst.

When we remember *that time*, we remember only the pain. The embarrassment, the regret, the trigger. We tend not to remember the lesson, the experience, the story. We don't remember that *that time* is why we never wear white bathing suits that are six years old (we throw those away). We remember not to use fake names because we've learned the guy on the date will eventually find out our real one, and that our British accent does not hold up when confronted with a real British person. We'll remember that SAT scores don't matter and half the things we said and did and wore are forgotten.

We've got to start reminding ourselves that our embarrassing experiences, our uncomfortable memories, aren't bad, but are nonthreatening parts of us that make up our colorful history. We have to remind ourselves that things can be awful, but that we survive and can come through them stronger, smarter, or at the very least, funnier.

In the 2006 comedy special *An Audience with Joan Rivers*, the comedienne tells the story of her husband's suicide. According to Rivers, the death of her husband was particularly traumatic because her fifteen-year-old daughter, Melissa, received the call from the police after they found him. After the death, the family sat shiva for a week and Joan could not find a way to connect with her daughter. Crying onstage, she tells the audience that when the shiva was over she took her daughter out to dinner in Beverly Hills in the hopes of reconnecting with her. But she still couldn't get through. She was scared her daughter would never be the same, their relationship forever altered, after such a scarring experience. So while at this famous restaurant they opened their menus and Rivers said, "Melissa, if Daddy were alive and saw these prices, he'd kill himself all over again." And her daughter laughed. And that's when Rivers said she got her daughter back.

Rivers built her career off using the unspoken and uncomfortable parts of life. In 1967 she talked about abortion on *The Ed Sullivan Show*. "I was the first one that dared to make jokes about it. And by making jokes about it, you brought it into a position where you could look at it and deal with it. It was no longer something that you couldn't discuss and had to whisper about. When you whisper about something, it's too big and you can't get it under control and take control of it, and that's what I still do."

And for the really bad memories, the ones that can't be turned into an anecdote or funny story, the ones we carry around like poison, well, those are the ones that connect us most deeply with others. Those, when we have the courage to share them, are what make us human. In the words of Grace Paley, "Sometimes you find that what is most personal is also what connects you most strongly with others."

We've survived everything we've faced. For better or worse, we've come out the other side, again and again. Yet we still doubt our abilities when the time comes. As a writer, I'm drawn over and over again to Nora Ephron's famous line "Everything is copy." The concept being that the worst things that happen make for the best stories. Only when we tell the stories later—the time our apartment flooded, the time we bombed on that presentation at work, the time we slipped on that banana peel—do we realize how insignificant, how inconsequential, and how funny those moments that felt like the end of the world really were.

Everything is copy is my new mantra when I'm thinking about the past and all those mistakes and embarrassing moments. Good stories are worth way more than nice experiences. Good stories are the reason people like to talk to you. For me, good stories pay the rent. I don't worry anymore about the moments I can't control. I don't worry about that thing I said or did. Instead, I thrive in my blunders and my mishaps. Sometimes, I even secretly hope for them.

SEE STRESS AS A CHALLENGE

> I've always been absolutely terrified every single moment of my life and I've never let it stop me from doing a single thing I wanted to do. —Georgia O'Keeffe

If we can see the past as funny and the future as inevitable, then the last milestone of anxiety, our mood, is how we see stress. Stress has always been a trigger for me. Things others see as benign, I see as stressful—group dinners, meeting Jay's parents for the first time, calling out sick from work. Stress occurs in the past, present, *and* future. Stress, unfortunately, is just part of life.

There came a point in my career when I was asked to attend a conference in Las Vegas. I was told I'd be there with another employee, Sandra. We'd never met because she worked remotely from San Diego.

"What's she like?" I asked my boss.

"She's great," she said.

"How old is she?" I asked, trying to imagine who I'd be hanging out with in the dry desert of Nevada for the next five days. Was she thirty? Did she have kids? Or was she some newly hired twentysomething they expected me to babysit?

"She's seventy-five," she said.

A week later I sat in the restaurant we'd planned to meet at the day before the conference. I'd gotten there early, figuring I'd make it easy on her and be the one on the lookout. How many seventy-five-year-olds would be walking around Vegas? When she introduced herself I was looking straight ahead toward the door. I'd been so focused on spotting an older woman that I didn't notice the petite blonde with the large blue eyes bounding toward me. "You must be Lauren," she cooed, extending her hand.

Two margaritas later, I told her what I'd wanted to say when she introduced herself. "You can't be seventy-five."

"Believe it, baby," she said.

"You look incredible. I can't believe you have seven grand-children."

She didn't seem embarrassed or amused, but like she'd heard it a million times. "You're only seventy-five if you want to be seventy-five," she said.

"No, but really, what's your secret?" I asked.

She looked at me point blank. "No stress." She took another sip of her margarita.

"What do you mean, no stress?"

"I mean, I never stress. I've been like this since maybe thirty-five. Something just happened and it clicked. I don't see *things* as things I have to do, but things I get to do."

Everyone always says that worrying creates lines. That stress ages. I always thought it was another way to make women feel bad. *Don't stress, you'll look ugly.* Turns out the woman who discovered just how stress affects the aging process ended up winning a Nobel Prize for it. Elizabeth Blackburn is a biological researcher whose study of telomeres and their effects on aging opened up an entire field of research and the way we understand the aging process.

To truly understand why stress makes you age, you need to understand how the body and, specifically, your telomeres work. The body is made up of billions of cells. Inside each cell are your chromosomes, which house your DNA. At the end of each chromosome is a "cap" known as a telomere. Like the plastic cap at the end of a shoelace, telomeres protect the chromosomes. Our cells, however, are constantly replenishing. Every time a cell divides, its DNA is copied to the new cell. But there is a glitch in the way DNA is copied. When a cell divides, some of the DNA gets worn down and shortened. Eventually the telomere, the protective cap on the chromosome, gets too short and falls off. When this happens, the cells stop dividing and replenishing.

It's these dying cells that make you look older and more prone to disease. Your hair goes gray because you have fewer pigment cells. You get wrinkles because you have fewer collagen cells. You get sick because you have fewer immune cells. But there was a ray of hope in all this research. We have some control over how fast our telomeres shorten and fall off. Blackburn discovered an enzyme called telomerase which can add DNA to the ends of chromosomes to slow and sometimes even reverse the aging process. According to Blackburn, there are things we can do that directly affect our telomerase and telomeres that either prolong or speed up the aging process.

Partnering up with Elissa Epel, a psychologist with expertise in the effects of chronic stress on our mind's and body's health, they sought to understand what happens to telomeres in people who are constantly stressed. Epel had been studying mothers, specifically, mothers of children with a chronic condition.

Blackburn and Epel found that the more years the mother had been in this caregiving situation, no matter her age, the shorter her telomeres were. And the more she perceived her situation as being stressful, the shorter her telomeres got still. Yet some mothers, despite having been carefully caring for their children for many years, had been able to maintain their long telomeres. Unlike the other mothers in the group, they did not lose the length of their telomeres even in the same stressful situation. When Epel researched the source of this difference it came down to one simple thing: These women did not perceive their situation as stressful, but as a challenge.

If you're habitually a negative thinker, you typically react to a stressful situation with a threat stress response. For example, if your boss calls you into her office, you might immediately think it's because you're getting fired. Your blood vessels constrict and your level of the stress hormone cortisol creeps up and stays up—even when it turns out your boss just wanted to check in. Over time, that persistently high level of cortisol damps down your telomerase, the enzyme that prevents the shortening of telomeres. On the other hand, if you typically see something stressful as a challenge to be tackled, then blood flows to your heart and your brain and you experience a brief but energizing spike of cortisol. And that is just fine for your telomeres. **By viewing stress as a challenge, rather than a threat, you can maintain your telomeres and live a longer, healthier life.**

It's a small shift in perspective that, like a new language, becomes ingrained over time. It's what Sandra had tried to explain when she said she didn't "have" to do things, but "got" to do them.

When it came to writing, I remember waking up Sunday mornings with a knot of fear at the bottom of my stomach. Knowing I had to spend the day working on the draft I didn't want to look at anymore, scared of how far I still had to go, how bad the writing from the day before was, was like perpetually having to face battle. And I'd avoid it, telling myself I was just going to watch one episode of *The Real Housewives* and take a walk, have lunch, or nap, and then begin. I avoided it because I was scared of it. And the fear and anxiety only increased as I'd try to distract myself, watching the minutes tick by until Jay would pop into the room and ask how it was going. "I haven't started yet," I'd tell him. Why not? "I'm scared."

But I had to get it done, scared or not. So instead of avoiding the project, I changed my perception of it. When I woke up in the morning, I made myself repeat the phrase "I'm excited to write. I'm excited to write." I'd pump myself up while at work, read-ing about other authors—quotes by them, advice from them—

remembering why I fell in love with writing to begin with. Just because writing was hard didn't mean it had to be scary. I began to look at it as a challenge to be tackled. Words to be found. Stories to be discovered. Slowly, my love for writing came back and the blank pages ahead felt less like a prison sentence and more like an adventure.

THE MOOD TRANSFORMED

I think I feel better. I look at everything from the other end—instead of expecting all and being lowered into despair each time I get less, I expect nothing now and, occasionally, I get a little, and am more than a little happy.

—Susan Sontag

When a thing's gone, it's gone. It's over and done with.

—Katherine Mansfield, "Je ne Parle pas Français"

Forget about the past and what you've done because it's what you think you can do *next* that matters.

—Iris Murdoch

THE MOOD:

BEAUTY

Symptoms include: irritability, dramatization, increased sensitivity, and adverse reactions to Instagram.

THE MOOD DESCRIBED

I didn't want my picture taken because I was going to cry. I didn't know why I was going to cry, but I knew that if anybody spoke to me or looked at me too closely the tears would fly out of my eyes and the sobs would fly out of my throat and I'd cry for a week.

—Sylvia Plath, *The Bell Jar*

I feel profoundly alone, cut off, unattractive . . . I feel unloveable.

—Susan Sontag

—I'm in pain all the time.
—Where?
—Inside. I can't explain it.

—Clarice Lispector, *The Hour of the Star*
(trans. Giovanni Pontiero)

It was a Saturday morning and I had a pimple. I'd spent sixty dollars at the dermatologist to get a cortisone shot (because I get the kind of pimples you can't pop) but three days later it was just as red, just as big, and just as impossible to cover up. I thought about calling the dermatologist and demanding another shot, for free this time, but that would mean I'd have to leave the house again and I was in a very dark place.

After debating calling in sick, I'd had to spend nine long hours at work the day before—avoiding as many interactions as possible, dodging eye contact with coworkers, and running to the bathroom every half hour to assess the cover-up situation. I remembered sitting on the subway, willing the train to get to my stop, the minutes dragging on until I could finally take off the mounds of concealer, put on an oversize T-shirt, and be ugly in peace. It was exhausting. I couldn't do that again.

But Jay wanted to go out, specifically to his friend Jeremy's roof party in Queens. The idea of standing in natural light, spending four hours trying to discreetly hold a plastic cup in front of my chin, created a tightening in my chest. No way. I couldn't do it. Not again. I felt sick. I felt gross. I just wanted to curl up in bed and forget about myself. I was sad. But I was also angry. Angry that I didn't look like Gisele Bündchen. Angry at my f*cking dermatologist. Angry that I was wasting another Saturday in this funk.

I spent the morning in what my mother would refer to as a "stew," which I now believe is short for stupor—a state of near-unconsciousness or insensibility. Imagine a deflated balloon with the sensitivity of an inflated one. It was getting closer to the start of the party and I didn't know if I should tell Jay I couldn't go because of the pimple or because of the mood it had created. Obviously both were true, but which was less pathetic? I told him I couldn't go because I wasn't in the mood. He asked if it was because of the pimple.

"No, but good to know you were lying when you said it wasn't noticeable," I replied, the shock of the *p*-word temporarily jolting me out of my stupor.

"Oh my God, it's not noticeable! I just know because you always get like this when you have a f*cking spot!" (He's British.)

"Get like what?" I demanded.

"Miserable!"

"Well, maybe I wouldn't be so miserable if I knew you were honest with me when I asked you the first time!" I answered, aware that my argument made no sense (another side effect of this mood is the loss of all rational thought).

So he went to Jeremy's without me, but not before delivering the gut-wrenching line "You know, *this* is really unattractive." *This*, I believe, was referring to my vanity.

I wanted to answer back, to tell him it wasn't vanity at all. Couldn't he see that? That my obsession with looking in the mirror, fixing my hair, stressing over pimples wasn't because I loved myself, but just the opposite? That the pimple was just a physical manifestation of the self-hatred that coursed through my body as steadily and consistently as my own blood? How could I explain that on those days when I was just in a mood and he couldn't figure out why, it was most likely because I didn't like what I saw in the mirror that morning?

I couldn't. Even if I could, I knew he would tell me to get over myself. He'd tell me that an obsession with my looks, whether I find them bad or good, is still an obsession. He'd tell me that caring this much about a pimple was pathetic. And he'd be right. And it's where I believe this specific mood stems from—this tug and pull of knowing we shouldn't care about something so petty while also trying not to collapse in agony over it.

WHAT THE MOOD IS TELLING YOU

There is no agony like feeling ugly. No pain like that of an unflattering photo. In an instant, the world becomes a cruel, inhospitable place. Like a forlorn child on a sidewalk, you want to wail and scream and have someone, anyone, pick you up and take you home, somewhere nice and warm and welcoming. But you can't cry. You can't tell anyone what's really wrong because they'll put you back down on the sidewalk and kick dirt in your face. *That's not a real problem, stop being so vain.*

Instead, when they ask what's wrong, why you aren't the same chipper girl you were before seeing the photograph, you'll bow your head in shame, pushing your sunglasses closer to your brimming eyelids, and say, "Sorry, just in a weird mood." Or maybe, "Nothing, just don't feel great." And if they don't know you very well they'll ask if you think you're getting sick. And you'll say something like "No, I don't think so. Nothing serious, anyway.

Just didn't get enough sleep." But you'll really want to break down and finally admit aloud, *I look hideous and I want to die.*

Unlike physical pain, this is a pain you're embarrassed to admit to. So you swallow it, day after day until it becomes a throb you barely notice anymore, until something nicks it—a pair of jeans that no longer fit, a beautiful new coworker, a bad hair day—and the ache courses through your body with such force that you're crying or screaming or yelling or accusing the person nearest to you because you don't know how to properly deal with the pain you're in. And after you do that, after you cover the wound with some dull Band-Aid, apologize to those you embarrassed yourself in front of, and scorn yourself for being so ridiculous and petty, you try to go back to daily life, to rejoin the game, but it's not fun anymore. The clouds are still there and it's forever a little darker, a little less fun.

No woman escapes life without experiencing this darkness. I know because in 2016, Dove launched a study to find out if female anxiety and body image were linked.

Surveying more than 10,500 women from thirteen countries, *The Dove Global Beauty and Confidence Report* became the largest comprehensive study on self-esteem to date, and its findings were unsettling. In Japan, it found that 92 percent of women dislike their bodies, followed by 80 percent in the UK. Additionally, 85 percent of the women surveyed stated that they chose not to do important life activities—such as trying out for a team or spending time with loved ones—when they didn't feel good about how they looked.

I understood that too well. So much of my life was dictated by how confident I felt, and all my confidence stemmed from how good I thought I looked. Days were rare when I'd take that first look in the mirror at six a.m. and find my skin dewy, my hair shiny, and my body acceptable. And even when those days happened, and I walked out of the apartment brimming with confidence, Emily Ratajkowski would choose that day to get on the same subway car.

If I wasn't passing beautiful women on the subway, it was at cocktail parties, in yoga class, at Juice Generation, on HBO. I felt like I couldn't get through a day without swatting away feelings of inferiority. No matter how good I felt, that inevitable moment would come when I'd be reminded that someone else was prettier. That's half the mood, isn't it? Feeling fine, then encountering some reminder of your own inadequacies and falling into a pit of despair. It's a quick slip with a hard fall. Musician Florence Welch describes the phenomenon: "I can still come off stage with a crowd applauding and go back to sit alone in my room, scrolling through my phone until I've found enough things to make me really unhappy," she explains. "Unflattering paparazzi pictures are good for that."

According to the U.S. Department of Health and Human Services, dissatisfaction with our bodies may be part of the reason more women than men have depression. Shocking, but not surprising. We know that capitalism thrives off of women feeling bad about ourselves. We know that if we didn't see models and perfectly primped actresses on our billboards and in our magazines, commercials, TV shows, and websites, we wouldn't think of beauty as being so important.

We know that the media rarely show us diversity in height, weight, color, skin type, hair texture, and other physical traits, in order to shame us into buying products that will help us race toward a homogeneous idea of beauty. We know all the sad facts and hard truths. Unfortunately, the truth alone does not set women free.

What does? Is it even possible for a woman to detach herself from her physical appearance? Is it possible to truly not care about what you see when you look in the mirror? Beauty is so abstract it's almost impossible to get a conclusive answer; however, there was one study that gave me hope. In 2015, professor Viren Swami of Anglia Ruskin University and academics from Sapienza University of Rome surveyed 484 Italian women, half mothers, half nonmothers, on how they felt about themselves and their bodies. Sixty-nine percent of the women who weren't mothers reported breast size dissatisfaction, a symptom associated with perfectionistic self-presentation. Interestingly, the same results were not found in the surveyed women who were mothers.

Those who had given birth had higher self-esteem about their breasts and a lower probability of suffering from perfectionistic self-presentation. And this is not because their breasts got bigger when they were pregnant. According to Professor Swami, "the most relevant [reason] is that becoming a mother—and particularly the experience of breastfeeding—may focus women's attention on breast functionality as opposed to focusing on the aesthetics of breasts and the body."

If these women stopped feeling bad about their breasts after realizing what they were there for, I remember thinking as I read the article, then maybe I could stop feeling bad about the rest of myself once I realized what I was here for.

A few weeks later a friend sent a *New Yorker* article about how doctors were experimenting with giving terminally ill cancer patients controlled doses of LSD to curb their fear of death.

Under the influence of hallucinogens, said one researcher, patients "transcend their primary identification with their bodies and experience ego-free states...and return with a new perspective and profound acceptance." In interviews with the test subjects, one of the most important themes found between all of their "trips" was that the impediment of a body was gone along with their individual identity.

Like many random, seemingly unimportant moments in our lives, this article, combined with the research I'd been doing, unlocked a door in a part of my mind I couldn't open before. After years of falling into mild depressions after seeing a bad photograph, an unwanted zit, a wrong angle in the mirror, it clicked. I was a slave to my identity. It was my ego that was holding me in this limbo of self-hatred. And if I was ever going to get past this mood, I'd have to sever the attachment to my ego, not just my looks.

GO VISIT YOUR GRANDMOTHER

Oh, how I regret not having worn a bikini for the entire year I was twenty-six. If anyone young is reading this, go, right this minute, put on a bikini, and don't take it off until you're thirty-four.

—Nora Ephron, *I Feel Bad About My Neck*

Around this time, at the age of twenty-five, I came to the liberating yet terrifying conclusion that I was never really going to change how I looked. Of course, I'd keep trying—keep wasting paychecks on $200 highlights, then growing out the $200 highlights and calling it balayage, then dyeing my hair brown, getting bangs, growing out the bangs, then going back to the $200 highlights—but I knew, deep down, that no amount of highlights or skin creams or new bronzer would ever change anything.

This acceptance was the hardest part, but once I hit it, I was able to move on to the real work. I was on the lookout for ways to accept myself, and my first breakthrough came with a trip to see my grandmother. I was visiting her in Florida for a long weekend, something I tried to do once a year like a good granddaughter, and like every year, she fawned all over me. From the moment I walked through the door she told me how beautiful I was. How radiant. How absolutely stunning.

Then she brought me around to see all her friends. Door to door we knocked and said hello and they gushed over me, talking about my skin, my blond hair, my height. Before, when she'd take me on the same parade, when she'd introduce me as her "beautiful granddaughter" to her friends at the pool and in the dining room, I waved it off. These compliments were coming from people who were surrounded by walkers, age spots, and titanium hips. Of course I seemed beautiful to them; any young person would. Then it hit me. Why did it matter *why* they thought I was beautiful? Why was I discrediting their compliments? Why couldn't I see what they were trying to tell me, which was that it didn't matter that I had a zit on my chin or that I'd gained a few pounds, because in their eyes, I still had the most beautiful thing, the one thing they didn't have—youth.

I had been wasting so many years waving away their tokens of advice wrapped in praise. Because they weren't just telling me I was beautiful, they were telling me to enjoy it. Enjoy it because this is the most beautiful I'd ever be. Enjoy it because whether I had gained a few pounds, was breaking out, or my hair was the color of mud, I was still beautiful because I was young. This time, I let them remind me of this. This time, I understood they were trying to tell me what a seventy-five-year-old Bette Davis told Johnny Carson in an interview.

Johnny Carson: Are you a severe critic of yourself when you watch yourself?

Bette Davis: I loathe myself. I have never liked what I have done...

Johnny Carson: But you must be happy with some of your work.

Bette Davis: Now, when I'm removed and see some of them. I never could stand my face, of course. It was just one of those things. Directors kept me out of rushes because I'd be so depressed for days.

Johnny Carson: What didn't you like about your face?

Bette Davis: I thought it was hideous! I couldn't stand it. Well now I'm a great many years older and I see some of those films and I don't think there's any question, I was the best-looking woman in the world.

The concept of appreciating what you have while you have it is not a new one. The principal theme of Buddhism and all these meditation apps we keep downloading is to learn how to be present in the moment. How to find harmony in the spaces in between. How, as Buddhist monk Thich Nhat Hanh would say, to "wash dishes while washing dishes."

According to Hanh, we only hate doing the dishes when we're not actually doing them. Most of the discomfort in our life stems from the inability to be present, to appreciate the moment for what it is while we're in it. If we were present, if we didn't let our minds wander outside of the moment when we're standing at the sink, we would find doing the dishes a pleasant task. Because the act of washing dishes, of dipping our hands in warm, soapy water or letting the fresh water run out of a tap while cleaning up from a meal that satisfied and nourished us, is an overall pleasant human experience. If you can get into it, it's nice. It's meditative.

But we stop seeing that way because we're too busy wishing for something else. Wishing for a dishwasher. Wishing for a maid. Wishing for it to be tomorrow. Wishing for anything that isn't right now. And then, when the moment is over, when the years have passed and we can no longer wash our own dishes because we're too old or too weak or too sick, or are now washing for one when we used to wash for two, we'll wish we had that moment back. That pleasant moment of standing in our home, hands in warm water, bodies and hearts full, our whole life ahead of us, slowly washing dishes.

Like children, we seem to only want things when we can't have them. We want our looks after we've lost them. We long for our youth after we've grown out of it. We want the past when we're in the future. How many times will we have to be told *appreciate what you have while you have it* before we take heed? How many women have tried to help us, passing this knowledge to an uninterested audience? How many times will we miss the point?

Find a photo of yourself from two, four, five years ago. Seriously, go grab one right now. Look at it and tell me you don't admire yourself there. Tell me you don't see how beautiful and young you were. Tell me you don't feel that pang of regret for having wasted that part of your life feeling ugly.

This isn't about glorifying youth or yearning for your twenty-three-year-old waistline. It's an exercise in perspective. It's about refocusing on all the things you currently take for granted. Your health, your freedoms, your opportunities. So many times our moods are dictated by our inability to accept the moment for what it is. Or as Flannery O'Connor says, "to cherish the world at the same time that you struggle to endure it." This jolt from my grandmother shocked me into the present by giving me a glimpse of the future. A future where I realized I'd wasted the best years, or at least the youngest years, of my life fretting about the insignificant parts. When I'd look back, I wouldn't remember the pimples or the frizz or the weight, but that I was young and hadn't appreciated it.

STOP THINKING YOU KNOW
WHAT YOU LOOK LIKE

You're so used to your features, you forget
how beautiful you look to a stranger.

—Unknown

Only when I accepted the liberating fact that this was the youngest I'd ever be, that this was the best I'd ever look, did I realize
I didn't know what I even looked like. I thought I knew, but it
was just a vague, distorted picture made up of all the flaws I saw
when I looked in the mirror.

When I looked in the mirror I didn't see my eyes; I saw eyebrows that needed tweezing. I didn't see my mouth; I saw lips
that were too thin. I didn't see my face, just a combination of
problems. Then I walked away from the mirror and carried on
with my day. So what do I look like? I never knew. But I could
tell you everything that's wrong with me.

Every woman can. Every woman walks around with a loaded
gun of all the things she'd change about herself. It's always
there, ready to fire off should someone ask us. In an interview
with journalist David Hartman, Audrey Hepburn answers with
frightening speed and clarity exactly what she would change
about herself:

David Hartman: How comfortable are you watching yourself on the screen?

Audrey Hepburn: Terribly uncomfortable. Always have been. I've always gone to see my rushes because I felt I should, because I thought maybe there's something I can still correct. But I'm terribly particular of myself. I don't like what I see. That's why it's always such a miracle to me. Because if I've been successful, the audience, the people, see something that I don't see.

David Hartman: If you could change anything about yourself what would it be?

Audrey Hepburn: I'd like to have had smaller feet. I hate having big feet and my friends have pretty feet and wear such pretty shoes.

We have become so used to not just our faces, but the obsessions, yearnings, and flaws attached to them that we no longer have any accurate, unbiased reading of what we actually look like. We accept our own deluded thoughts as reality, when in fact the outside world sees something completely different. I didn't realize this, however, until I met Valerie.

Valerie and I worked together at one of my first jobs in New York. When she introduced herself to me on my first day I didn't let on that I already knew her because we'd gone to the same university.

I had first noticed her at one of the rare frat parties I attended, while sitting on a broken armrest of a putrid beige tweed couch, sipping warm beer, wondering if any of the guys doing a keg stand were boyfriend material.

Then I saw her. The guys around the keg had lifted her into the air, carrying her through the living room like a Greek goddess. Her orange Juicy sweatpants exposed a midriff toned a deep summer copper, the glint of her belly button ring catching the light of the living room's ceiling lamp. Her hair: long, brown, and shiny.

When they finally put her down, I saw her petite nose, high cheekbones, and perfectly arched eyebrows. I remember wanting to leave. To get out of that room with the perfect girl. Yet even when I did, the thoughts stayed, the thoughts I had the whole time while looking at her: *She must be so happy. She must be so happy.*

Those same thoughts flooded back five years later when I saw her on the first day of my new job.

Of course she's in New York. She probably has the best life. I bet she's going to the best parties. Has the best roommates. Goes on the best dates with the best guys.

At this point she'd ditched the Juicy sweats and was effortlessly pulling off black corduroys and crisp white collared blouses, which made the perfect canvas for her shoulder-length silky brown hair with soft caramel highlights naturally running through it. *So chic. So French.* So when she asked me to grab a drink with her after work I accepted excitedly in anticipation of seeing the beautiful life of this beautiful girl. I wasn't even jealous. Just curious.

The first shock came when we stopped at her apartment to grab a coat. The five minutes she told me it would take turned into fifty. She'd been running back and forth between the bathroom and her bedroom while I sat, holding my phone, watching her change from a silky green strappy tank to a silky *blue* strappy tank. Happy hour was ending soon and I was getting impatient.

"Valerie?" I called toward the bedroom.

"So sorry! I just can't figure out what to wear. I hate everything I own. I'm so fat."

"What? You're crazy. You didn't even have to change from what you wore to work. I thought you looked great."

Her laugh had a dark chill to it. "You're crazy," she said. "I looked disgusting today. Just five more minutes, I promise!" Ten minutes later we left. Valerie was wearing a black leather skirt instead of the black corduroys and the same crisp white collared top.

When we got to the bar we found two empty seats and rushed for them. Next to us were four guys. Both of us were single, and I thought how fortuitous it was that Valerie was with me. We could bait the good guys for once. I waited for her to make a move. To give permission to the handsome men sneaking glances at her.

"Hey, ladies." The words came from the back of my head. I swiveled around to see a sweaty, tanned twenty-something wearing a black muscle shirt, exposing an inch of chest hair. His black locks were matted beneath a backward Mets hat.

"Hi," we said back, simultaneously.

"Let me guess, PR?" He leaned in closer, smiling, like he'd just made the funniest, wittiest remark in the history of the world.

"Um, no. I'm a writer. She's an editor," I replied, offended and hoping he'd notice.

"But it may as well be PR," Valerie's voice echoed next to me, as she smiled at him. *Um, what?* I swiveled my chair to look at her, hoping to catch some glimmer in her eye, some denotation that she was, in fact, messing with him.

"I thought so." He leaned in closer.

He smelled of nachos and vodka tonic. *Oh, I see. She's just going to get some free drinks out of this guy. Fine, I'll indulge him for five more minutes*, I told myself.

Five minutes passed and they continued talking and no drinks had been bought. Instead I watched Valerie give him her number. After he left and before I could ask her what that was all about, she ordered herself a tequila shot and opened her purse to look for some lipstick.

When she found it she started applying it with an open compact mirror in the other hand, speaking to me as if we were best friends in a bathroom. "I saw the most beautiful girl walking down the street last week. It put me in a depression for three days." She closed the compact.

"What?" I knew I was staring at her now, trying to make sure I wasn't missing something. *How could anyone be more beautiful than you?* I thought.

"I'm thinking of getting lip fillers," she continued, "and obviously a boob job when I have the money."

"What? Why?" I asked aloud.

"I just hate myself," she replied. It was less of an answer and more of a declaration. As if she'd been waiting to get it off her chest. I was stunned. *What? Valerie hates herself? But how can she hate herself if I'd give my right arm to look like her?*

I continued to stare at her, trying to make sense of what she was saying. *Okay, she doesn't have lips like Angelina Jolie and she's no Brigitte Bardot, but she's still beautiful.* In fact, I hadn't noticed her small boobs or "thin" lips, I just saw her as a whole package, as pretty Valerie with her high cheekbones, good skin, and hazel eyes.

By the time I wrapped my mind around what she was saying, she'd ordered a second tequila shot. And by the time I got her in a cab an hour later, I realized that everything I thought I understood about myself and beauty was all wrong.

If Valerie couldn't see herself clearly, maybe no woman could. Or maybe Valerie was just crazy. Or maybe we all are. Or maybe who cares? I suddenly hated myself for thinking about it so much. Who cares if I'm pretty or I'm not! I felt like screaming half the time.

STOP SELF-CHERISHING

I have already settled it for myself so flattery
and criticism go down the same drain and I
am quite free.

—Georgia O'Keeffe

I do care. Then I don't. Then I do. Then I go on a spree at Sephora because new foundation and thirty-dollar eyeliner is what's been keeping me from true beauty. Then I don't care and go a week without washing my hair. Then I care again and want to look French. Then I go broke buying an overpriced Chanel beret that will sit in my closet for years because I can't actually pull it off.

Then I hate myself for spending so much money on a beret and *boom*, the mood is back.

The snap occurs when the tension between the two opposing thoughts becomes too tight. When the mind is trying to tell you not to care about something so trivial, so superficial, while also wishing so badly for it. When the anger and disappointment with yourself well up to an unmanageable level.

The Buddhists might say this feeling is created through self-cherishing and that self-cherishing is the root of all suffering. Self-cherishing sounds positive, but it's more like self-obsessing. It is a mindset that arises from believing that we are the center of the universe and that our specific desires, goals, and wishes are the most important. In his book *How to Transform Your Life: A Blissful Journey*, Buddhist monk Kelsang Gyatso described self-cherishing: "First we develop the thought, 'I am important,' and because of this we feel that the fulfillment of our wishes is of paramount importance... Then we desire for ourself that which appears attractive and develop attachment, we feel aversion for that which appears unattractive and develop anger, and we feel indifference toward that which appears neutral and develop ignorance."

By being overly aware of ourselves, of what we look like, what we have, or what we don't have, we stifle and block ourselves. We create this tension, this awkward self-awareness, and are unable to move and function with ease. We become obsessed with our outer selves and lose our authentic selves. It's a constant state of fixation leading to the millions of things we do to try to appease ourselves, make ourselves feel better, that keep us locked in a cycle of unfulfillment.

These fixations aren't just on our looks. They are on everything we think will keep us happy and keep negative feelings, like unworthiness or shame or fear, away. It's the cars and the schools and the Instagram pictures we keep obsessing over, throwing ourselves at, only to find ourselves in a deep hole with more followers, more debt, more stuff.

Self-cherishing is why every time I got a pimple I fell into a mood. The pimple was an obstruction of my desire for perfection. I believed that I should have flawless skin so anytime something reminded me that I didn't, or couldn't, I freaked out. My problem wasn't the blemish, but the feelings it brought. The feelings of inadequacy, shame, and fear. But these feelings were just by-products of my obsession with myself.

The Buddhists believe the antidote to self-cherishing is in practicing selflessness. By focusing on the needs of others, we can start to let go of our own selfish desires. Tonglen, a Tibetan word meaning "sending" (tong) and "receiving" (len), is a healing practice that awakens compassion and over time, helps stop the cycle of self-cherishing.

Originally used in meditation, many teachers have adapted the technique to be used anytime, anywhere, to train students in the habit of facing their suffering and opening their hearts. The instructions are simple: With every breath in, you are to take in the pain of others, and with every breath out, you send relief. When you begin to feel sorry for yourself, when you feel your wishes are not being met, when you come face-to-face with suffering, you breathe in the pain, not just your own, but the pain of anyone you can think of who is also suffering. After inhaling it like smoke, you breathe out a blessing. A prayer. Good thoughts for all of those you wish to heal.

The point of tonglen is to turn a moment of selfish obsession into connection. To use our suffering as a cue to be present with our pain and transform it into compassion. To awaken our sense of the world around us. To remind us that we are not alone, in our pain and joy, and that by connecting with others, we can feel less alienated by our problems.

When I started feeling unattractive—when I looked in the mirror and hated my greasy hair and the rosacea covering my face—I didn't turn away from my reflection, but thought of all the other women I knew feeling the same way. All the women staring at their stretch marks and pockmarks and scars and breathed in their pain. I breathed in as deep as I could, as long as I could, as if the longer and deeper I held it the more women I could touch, and when I couldn't hold it any longer, I breathed out relief. I breathed out hope that they found comfort and beauty in themselves. I breathed out acceptance and compassion and confidence. I breathed out everything I wanted for myself and gave it to them.

The more I did this, the less irritable I became. The less alone I felt in my suffering. Eventually, like the Buddhists suggested, I found myself doing this not just when I confronted my own pain, but when I saw pain in others. When a baby started wailing in the middle of a crowded restaurant in Brooklyn, instead of judging the mother for bringing a baby to a nice restaurant, I breathed in her stress and sent out peace for her.

In a way, it was a practice of manifestation. By putting into the universe blessings for others, I was increasing the good energy around me. I was turning negatives into positives. Turning the feeling of ugliness, inadequacy, and shame into beauty.

STOP LOOKING IN MIRRORS

You can be absolutely wonderful looking in
person and not photograph well.

—Lauren Hutton

I want to do an experiment. I have it all planned out. I just
need a private island and no mirrors. I know the island sounds
excessive, but I've thought this through and there's really no
other way. Have you ever tried to use a public restroom without looking in the mirror? Or passed a car without noting
your reflection in the window? Or gotten into an elevator and
not looked up or down or into the shiny doors that close? It's
impossible.

The plan is to live a year without coming into contact with any
reflective surfaces. No cell phones, no glass buildings, no silver
faucets, no crystal ponds, nada. Not one thing that I can look
at or into. This includes people. I don't want to walk into a bar
and start deducing from the attention or inattention of the guy
sitting next to me whether I look attractive or not. I don't want
to analyze the glances of a passing stranger or talk to someone
and wonder if they're staring at a loose piece of hair or an escaped
booger. I don't want to see myself in the eyes of anyone. I don't
want to see myself at all. Period.

In this time I believe I will reach a state of transcendence where my thoughts are free to roam, no longer attached to the heavy weight of beauty. Where I lose all concept of self-awareness and experience presence. Where I am just me. Not me with over-processed hair. Not me with bad skin. Not me with untweezed eyebrows.

After a year of isolation I will return to normal society and for the first time in 365 days, look into a mirror. And I believe I will see myself as more beautiful than I ever have before. I will see myself as a mother sees her child, a one-of-a-kind gift. I will see all the amazing features I've overlooked after years of giving all my attention to the "flawed" ones. I will see what it means to be beautiful.

Obviously, this private island plan can only happen with lots of money and resources, so in the meantime I've found the second-best thing to do is to avoid the other type of mirror—social media.

If you want to remove yourself from your ego, you may need to eventually remove yourself from Instagram. I know, it's like saying you need to eat kale or go to the gym more. We've heard it, we know it, we don't want to do it.

But we can't continue living this way, hoping for change so radical that there's no conceivable way to achieve it. And if you're not going to go to the gym (which I don't), meditate (which I didn't even bring up because we've all heard it and get it by now), or eat more salmon (which gets expensive), you need to do something else. And to me, posting less on social media seemed like the easiest way out.

I always had a vague feeling that every selfie I posted was, as Susan Sontag believes, taking a part of my soul. But the rush of a good hair day and ideal lighting was always so addictive. Like any drug, however, the comedown came on fast. As soon as I'd uploaded a photo I'd be hit with a wave of anxiety, wondering about how many people would like it, if the right people would like it, if it came off as vain, trying too hard. If deleting it would be weird. The photo I'd put up because I thought I looked great had now produced the opposite effect. And apparently, I wasn't alone.

In 2018, Jennifer S. Mills, Sarah Musto, Lindsay Williams, and Marika Tiggemann performed a study designed to test whether taking and posting selfies elicited change in mood and body image among women. Enlisting 110 female undergraduate students from York University in Toronto, Canada, they assigned the women to one of three groups:

Group 1: Taking and posting an untouched selfie

Participants were asked to take a single photo (a head shot) on the lab's iPad and upload it to their preferred social media profile (Facebook or Instagram).

Group 2: Taking and posting a retouched and preferred selfie

Participants were asked to take one or more photos of themselves on the lab's iPad and were told that they could use the photo-editing app installed on the iPad to retouch the photo to their satisfaction before uploading it to their social media profile.

Group 3: No posting of selfies

Participants were given the lab's iPad but were asked to read a short article from a social media news website chosen for neutral, non-appearance-related content (i.e., popular travel ideas for university students) and to answer questions about the article.

The participants were evaluated on their moods before and after the experiment. As predicted, the women who posted selfies in the first two groups reported feeling more anxious, less confident, and more physically unattractive than the women who did not upload selfies.

In fact, the mean level of anxiety between when they walked into the study and when they left it increased by 10 percent for the women who posted the untouched selfies and 5.5 percent for the retouched group. Meanwhile, anxiety decreased by 5 percent for the control group asked to read an article and answer questions about it.

Besides the anxiety, confidence dropped 15 percent for the untouched selfie group and 7 percent for the retouched group. Researchers believe that this is because women typically react to seeing a photo of themselves by feeling dissatisfied with their appearance.

And why wouldn't we? We see so much crap, or rather, "beauty," on social media all day long that we're conditioned to feel disappointed. It's model, hot girl from college you don't remember following, model, a picture of pancakes, model, baby, baby, model, your beautiful high school friend with the crema filter.

Social media is a microcosm of life. It's a summary of all your illusions, hopes, dreams, anxieties, and fears. But if you only see models and engagement photos and beautifully filtered friends out to dinner without you, your world becomes as small of those things.

At a certain point, my Instagram feed became a source of anxiety. My heart would thump a little faster when I clicked on the icon or opened Facebook. Because the only content I was ingesting was content that made me feel bad about myself. But I wasn't ready to get off Facebook or Instagram. They were how I communicated. How I stayed in touch. I was too depressed to keep scrolling but too weak to leave.

So I started an Instagram account that would make me feel better while on the app. It would be a quiet revolution to disrupt the feed. I would create captivating images that stopped women midscroll, and while I had their attention, I would give them some thought or lesson or truth so powerful, so fascinating, so honest, that they'd forget their momentary anxiety. They'd be shocked out of their daze and brought back into reality, or rather, into meaning.

Anything I found that made me feel better, that made me think about something differently, that made me forget myself or like myself or understand myself, was posted. They were stories about women that made me excited to be a woman. Reminders and lessons, advice and wisdom. I thought that maybe if we could just keep looking at content like this, content that was never about women's looks but about their stories, successes, eccentricities, intelligence, experience, honesty, and integrity, we could forget about beauty and become obsessed with finding these qualities in ourselves.

I didn't know when I started Words of Women that our brains have a built-in negativity bias. That we build and deepen and strengthen neural pathways that make us feel bad about ourselves.

I didn't know that your brain is predisposed to remember and prioritize bad memories; that if we don't actively work on ourselves, these negative thoughts will dominate our lives. When I found all that out I realized there was an even bigger purpose to Words of Women.

It wasn't just about making women feel something good while scrolling on Instagram, it was about making women change the way they thought about everything they saw on Instagram. It was about introducing a new way of thinking and being. And with enough time, enough images, enough newsletters, enough articles, enough information, we could rewire our brains to see not just ourselves but our lives in a more positive light.

YOU'RE NOT PRETTY LIKE HER, YOU'RE PRETTY LIKE YOU

You know, there's a thing about the woman across the room. You see the woman across the room, you think, She's so poised; she's so together. But she looks at you and you are the woman across the room for her.

—Diane von Furstenberg

Why do we only remember the bad? Why do we get ten compliments and only remember the one negative remark? Why can't we remember the time someone called us beautiful but still remember when Rebecca from accounting made a snide comment about our shoes?

Because the brain functions from old reptilian patterns that are hardwired to remember the bad or threatening. According to psychology professor Elizabeth Kensinger, when we have an emotional reaction to a negative event—being broken up with, getting mugged, someone's death—we remember those details with vivid clarity because "the emotional circuitry in the brain kind of turns on and enhances the processing in that typical memory network such that it works even more efficiently and even more effectively." We're storing negative moments in order to learn from them, to be able to recognize the triggers and avoid the situation in the future.

It's why you'll never forget the first guy or girl who ghosted you. The first time something like that happens, you imprint it. And because you'll never forget it, you now know what to watch out for next time you're talking to someone new. You know what signs to look for.

These moments, these bad memories, build and strengthen our inherent negativity bias. Our brain consists of pathways that are a lot like streams that can get bigger or stronger with use. Every time we process an experience, it goes down either the negative or the positive pathway, emptying out into our personal interpretation.

Nine times out of ten, our reality—which is made up of comments, thoughts, and observations—is coming in and getting sucked right down the negativity pathway because that one is stronger. We don't even get a choice about how we perceive a comment, a reaction, an encounter. The negative stream is so strong, its current so forceful.

Besides the fact that we swim this path every day, making it stronger and deeper, there's the fact of evolution and our initial wiring. We still have parts of the brain that exist the same way they do in other animals. We still have fight-or-flight mode—a function that's only here because of our ancestors.

And this part of our brain tries to protect us by coding negative memories with permanence. It's why we remember that one negative comment instead of the sea of one hundred amazing ones. It's why we lie awake going over all the bad memories and moments of our past instead of the good ones.

But evolution also gave us new parts of the brain and ways to use our intelligence to fight back against the reptilian brain. One of those ways is cognitive awareness—paying close attention to when we're pushing thoughts, comments, memories down the negative stream and actively seeking to override it. To push the thought onto the other path. To work day after day on widening and strengthening the small trickle that is the positive stream into a current as strong and forceful as the negative one.

One of the ways you build this positive flow is by reinforcing it with positive messages. One message that changed my course of thinking was *You're not pretty like her, you're pretty like you.* I don't remember where or when I saw it, but like so many of the quotes and small phrases I heard or observed throughout my life, it stuck with me. It stuck with me so much that I made it into a sticker. And then I put that sticker on the back of my phone. And that sticker was there when I got on the subway and I saw a beautiful girl. And when that sinking feeling started to grab hold of me and I'd almost automatically start obsessing over all the things she had that I didn't, I trained myself to look at that sticker. *You're not pretty like her. You're pretty like you.*

When I looked at that sticker I felt better. I'd think of all the people who loved me. All the beautiful things people said to me over the years. I thought of all my unique qualities. My talents. My individual beauty. I thought it, saw it, and said it enough times that when I got a new phone and lost the sticker, I didn't need it anymore. I knew it then. It was automatic. It popped into my brain when I passed billboards and celebrities and pretty girls on the street. And it didn't just make me feel better, it made me less judgmental. I was able to appreciate another woman's beauty and mine at the same time.

THE MOOD TRANSFORMED

The first feminist gesture is to say: "OK, they're looking at me. But I'm looking at them." The act of deciding to look, of deciding that the world is not defined by how people see me, but how I see them.

—Agnès Varda

How simple life becomes when things like mirrors are forgotten.

—Daphne du Maurier, *Frenchman's Creek*

You don't have to be born beautiful to be wildly attractive.

—Diana Vreeland

THE MOOD:

WORK

Symptoms include: agitation, restlessness, and a desire to move to the Bahamas and sell handmade bracelets.

THE MOOD DESCRIBED

I awoke this morning tired and sad. Feeling
physically inadequate before the day, feeling
like closing my eyes again.

—Anaïs Nin

I discovered that I am tired of being a person.

—Susan Stonag, *I, etcetera*

And all day I've been like a whirlwind inside—

—Georgia O'Keeffe

It was a warm Thursday in July and getting out of bed felt impossible. The sheets were sticking to my leg and my face was under the duvet, avoiding the white light pouring through the window. Jay had just drawn the curtains—after making a smoothie and coffee and probably catching up on a few emails. Sometimes I thought he was a robot. The way he naturally woke up. The way he jumped into the shower, then straight into jeans. The way he was always ready to go. I, on the other hand, was exhausted before I began. I had to find the energy to get out of bed, and that morning it felt particularly difficult.

At seven thirty, I tried to push myself out of it. Standing up, stretching, and walking to the bathroom, I focused on the tasks ahead of me. I brushed my teeth, washed my face, and put on deodorant in automatic succession. Only, this morning I was taking my time, trying to avoid Jay as much as possible because I didn't have the energy to act normal, happy. We were at a fragile point in our relationship and I knew if he sensed something was wrong it would lead to something bigger.

It would lead to something bigger because I wasn't supposed to be in a bad mood, at least not right now. It hadn't even been two months since I quit my job at the marketing company I thought was making me miserable, and taken half the salary to work as my father's assistant. I'd told Jay that if I had more time to work on my book, I wouldn't be so stressed all the time. I'd also told him that if I didn't have to commute I wouldn't be so miserable by the time I got home. I told him it was for my mental health. Though he argued that joining the family business was the opposite of what a mentally healthy person would do, he agreed to pay half my rent, and in return, I was supposed to be happier. But that morning I didn't feel happy.

Once I heard the front door close, I sucked in some air and began my routine of washing the blender, unloading then reloading the dishwasher, making the bed, and straightening up the pillows on the couch. It was implied that I would take care of the housework, so even though I was supposed to be working less, I'd picked up the additional jobs of chef and maid.

After straightening up, I set up my laptop on the kitchen island to begin work. Upon opening my computer, I felt a familiar tightening in my stomach, the same white rage I had felt when I sat down to work at my last job. The same disdain for everything. Only this time it was for my apartment. The construction site outside my window. The way the smell of the trash wafted up from the bin next to the kitchen island.

I started thinking about how I hated working from home. How not seeing anyone for eight hours was unnatural. How I didn't have anyone to commiserate with. How at least I'd had coworkers to complain to at my last job. Now I only had my dad. And the last time I'd tried to complain to him I ended up getting a call from my mother about how I needed to "act professional" if this job was ever going to work. So not only did I not have coworkers to speak to, but I wasn't speaking to my mother either.

I worked straight through until one, stopping only to make

a sandwich and walk around the apartment to look for the air-conditioning remote. Around two, it was time to shut off from my dad's job and start working at the other, my writing. I switched from the kitchen island to the desk in the bedroom. After three hours and less than two pages, I decided to call it quits. It was already five and I needed to go to the grocery store and get out of the mood before Jay came home. But instead of getting out of it, I fell deeper in.

Whole Foods was rammed and four of the ingredients I needed for my chicken recipe were out of stock. Should I scrap the recipe or try to scrape by without the ingredients? If I changed the recipe, what would I make? Was I supposed to get toilet paper? The questions flew across my brain, swirling into a cloud of rage. I hated Whole Foods. I hated that I always forgot something. I hated that life felt so heavy and hard even though I knew it wasn't. I hated that I was in this mood.

I ended up getting toilet paper we didn't need and forgetting the essential chicken for the recipe. This realization, made with my head inside the refrigerator, sent tears flying. Hot, thick tears that quickly turned into heaving. Wailing. A good old-fashioned purging. This was it, I thought, I was expelling the mood. Only, when I'd calmed down, blotting my eyes with toilet paper and examining my face in the mirror like I always did after a good cry, I didn't feel relieved. The knot was still there, and dinner, I remembered, wasn't. I debated texting Jay and asking him to pick up the chicken on his way home. But that wasn't part of our agreement. Besides, by the time he got home it would be almost seven. So I put my coat back on, walked the five blocks back to Whole Foods, and with red, puffy eyes bought the damn chicken.

It was raining by the time I walked out, that warm, summer rain that smells of concrete, and every step I took back toward the apartment felt like a step toward the end. I checked my phone and noticed a few new work emails. Even though I knew I was off the clock I felt a tightening in my chest. *How dare these people email me now. How dare they ask for something after work hours.* I knew I didn't have to respond until tomorrow, yet the idea of them sitting there, waiting for me, sent me further into despair. The mood that had started as a small tight ball that morning was now a black hole, and I was standing on the edge of it. The wrong look from Jay could set me off. Another work email could throw me into hysterics. A loud truck rattling down the street could topple me. My mind was racing, going through all the things I could do to get rid of this mood. The last-ditch efforts. Drink. Smoke. Scream. Cry. Run. Watch TV. Something, anything to calm me down, relax me, neutralize me. But none of it felt like the right thing. I wanted everything and nothing.

"What's wrong?" Jay asked five minutes after arriving home. He must have sensed it by the way I squeaked out a "Hey" as he walked through the door. Trying to sound cheerful and light was like trying to lift a hundred-pound weight. Or maybe he saw how tightly my wrist was whisking the marinade. Or maybe he saw it in my eyes, the wild look they had in them.

"Nothing," I replied. "Just a bad day at work."

WHAT THE MOOD IS TELLING YOU

Was it work? Was it even a bad day? It wasn't my ideal day, sitting by a pool on the Amalfi Coast, but nothing terrible had happened. A few annoying emails. A few trips to the grocery store. A failed chicken recipe. Not only was nothing actually wrong, but I'd eliminated all the things I thought were wrong with the last job. The commute. The long days. That four o'clock hour when I'd finished yet had to stay in my seat until exactly five thirty. None of that was my issue anymore. So why did this feel like the same mood I'd get when I used to have to do all that?

I tried to describe it by writing it out in my notepad. "Exhausted. Irritated. Restless." *Forget it*, I thought. I was too drained to be doing more work. I threw my pen and journal back into my drawer and finished the bottle of wine on the counter to knock myself out. It had been a terrible day and I still didn't know why.

It took me a while to understand what this mood was telling me. I experienced the sensation of it at least five more times, until a few weeks later a friend shared an article that had nothing to do with work yet described everything I was feeling about it. It was about willpower, self-control, and a psychological theory known as ego depletion.

The theory posits that willpower is a finite resource. Like energy or strength, the more willpower we use throughout the day, the less we have later. It's why you find it harder to go to the gym after work. It's why you're more agitated and irritable in the middle of the week as opposed to the beginning. It's why you have less patience with your parents toward the end of their visit, even though they're no more judgmental or neurotic than when they first arrived.

The theory of ego depletion was first conceived by social psychologists Roy Baumeister and Mark Muraven. Their lab conducted multiple studies to measure the self-control of individuals after completing tasks that required them to exert willpower. In one study participants spent several minutes listing whatever thoughts came into their minds. One group of participants, however, was told that they could think about anything except a white bear. After the exercise, participants were given a set of anagrams to solve. These anagrams were unsolvable, yet Baumeister measured how long subjects tried before giving up. The participants who had to suppress the white bear thought gave up significantly faster than people not forced to regulate their thoughts.

The same type of experiment was performed measuring willpower levels after resisting. They found participants who were put in a room and told not to eat a plate of cookies in front of them spent only eight minutes trying to solve the puzzle compared to the twenty-one minutes the group that wasn't given a plate of cookies to restrain against spent working on the anagram. It was clear that a pattern was emerging: The more we suppress the stuff we want and do the stuff we don't want to do, the less self-control we have later.

Imagine your willpower and self-control as a tank of gas. A full tank enables you to operate at optimal performance, to be the kind, patient, motivated person you want to be. It keeps you going to the gym because you made a promise to yourself. It keeps you from snapping at your coworkers because as angry as you are, you know their loyalty is more important. It keeps you from ordering McDonald's because you know a healthy dinner will make you feel better later.

By midweek, two-thirds of that gas is gone and you begin to feel the strain of it. You no longer have the motivation to go to the gym. You start having less patience with clients and find it harder to get through the commute without screaming. Soon, you're running on empty. So when you finally walk through your door and look at the healthy leftovers in the fridge, you can't help but pour yourself a shot of Tito's and order a pizza. Then you get bored in your apartment because this is the time you allotted for the gym, or journaling, or doing any of the other healthy habits you said you'd start building, so you walk to your neighborhood bar and drink to forget about everything you should be doing. And at this bar you'll meet Jim, who will have a charming smile and, you'll eventually find out, chlamydia. But that's not the point. The point is that **ego depletion is the crux of most women's irrational behavior**—whether we're working nine to five or not.

This mood wasn't due to my job; this mood was depletion. The result of continuous action and forced suppression. It didn't matter where I was working because it wasn't about the job but the effort it took to get through a day. The amount of willpower I used hadn't changed, just shifted tasks. Instead of commuting, I was cleaning. Instead of sitting at a desk, I was standing at Whole Foods. When I was depleted, I perceived and thought about the world around me differently, almost like being in a different emotional state. When I was depleted, life felt harder.

Ego Depletion Is the Reason

We're Cranky When We're Tired

Have you ever thought about why we're cranky when we're tired? It's not that being tired makes you cranky. Being tired means you didn't get enough sleep, which means you didn't replenish your willpower and you're now forced to go about your day with a smaller amount of willpower, making every task seem harder, every impulse stronger, and every judgment obscured. Your brain is foggy because it's working from a depleted state.

We Can't Curb Our Bad Habits

All of your bad habits are triggered by cues. Ever wonder why even though you said you'd quit smoking, you can't help bumming a cigarette on a night out? That's because alcohol, the city, the bars, the cues around you trigger the habitual response to smoke. When willpower is high, we can actively fight those triggers. We can force ourselves to acknowledge the cue and stop the habit. When we're depleted, however, our willpower is too low to fight the automatic habits triggered by these cues.

We Make Dumb Decisions

When we're feeling drained we're less likely to take the time to evaluate situations. We usually make our biggest mistakes when we're "too burned out" to do the necessary research. This was showcased in a study with parole officers by Jonathan Levav of the Stanford Graduate School of Business and Shai Danziger of Ben-Gurion University. In the beginning of the day, when the officers were more energized, they gave more time and energy to the cases they needed to review in front of them. By the end of the day, they spent less time getting to know prisoners and reviewing the cases. Analyzing more than 1,100 decisions over the course of a year, the study found that **prisoners who appeared early in the morning received parole about 70 percent of the time, while those who appeared late in the day were paroled less than 10 percent of the time.**

Depletion was about absence, and the more I noticed it, the more I realized how wrongly I'd been tending to it. Instead of finding ways to refill, I was squeezing every last drop out of myself. Instead of taking on less, I was taking on more. Instead of taking breaks, I was using spare moments to run errands. I was treating pain with pain. The same way my body told me it was tired at the gym, this mood was a signal my energy, my willpower, was low. A sign that I'd run myself too close to empty and I needed to replenish. If depletion was the mood, the solution was knowing how to refill the tank.

REGRETFULLY DECLINE

I restore myself when I'm alone.

—Marilyn Monroe

When we say things will be better in the morning, it's because sleep is one of the psychologically proven ways to restore will-power. But I didn't have the luxury to go to sleep every time I needed to restore myself. I needed to find ways throughout the day to keep my willpower from draining. One of those ways, I quickly realized, was to say no as often as I could.

I used to be the queen of accepting invitations. Not just formal invitations. Invitations to bridal showers and dinners and after-work drinks. Invitations to brunches with people I didn't like. Invitations to meet my cousins on their impromptu visit and show them around New York. Even if I didn't really want to accept, I always said yes. I felt bad saying no. The fear of letting other people down trumped my own desire to just lie down.

I didn't realize that saying no and feeling guilty is a lot better than saying yes and acting like a psycho. Saying no when you've had a long week and just need time to yourself on Saturday is the difference between having a meltdown in the Bloomingdale's Men's Department and not having one. (To be fair, this happened just a few days after my ego-depletion realization, when I thought

I was only depleted after work. I hadn't yet realized that depletion happens on the weekend too.)

I'll summarize. It was Saturday morning, two days after my Thursday mood, and even though it had been a long week, I agreed to go with Jay to buy a new suit. More specifically, his wedding suit. It had to be from Bloomingdale's because our friend worked there and could get us a discount. The problem with Bloomingdale's is it's in the middle of Manhattan, two trains and a transfer at Union Square from our Brooklyn apartment.

Because our wedding was in September, we had to get the suit by the end of July. This particular July was the hottest on record, and to celebrate, the MTA was doing renovations on the Brooklyn subway line. This meant the train only came every twenty minutes.

When we got to Bloomingdale's an hour later, I relished the air-conditioning and the temporary relief that the small twinge of angst I'd felt on the subway was subsiding. We found the suit section. We started looking. Jay started trying on. I watched. I gave my opinion. I carried the other sizes he wanted to try. I was a good fiancée, I thought to myself. I was a real grown-up.

I wasn't sure if the salespeople at Bloomingdale's made commission, but a sweet old saleslady had decided to follow us around to make sure she was there for it. I felt bad for her, standing on her feet all day. She had to be at least seventy. I tried to be extra nice, showing her a picture of my dress, making chitchat while Jay went to try things on. I really wanted her to leave us alone, but I figured I could make this woman's day either with a good commission or at least a friendly encounter.

Then we went to shoes. We asked to try three different pairs.

Along with the three in our price range, the saleslady brought out another pair, an expensive pair we'd never normally consider. But she told us that Ferragamo was for special occasions. I pointed out that Ferragamo was expensive. Then she pointed out that there is no price too high for quality.

"Is it worth spending more money on the shoes or the suit?" I asked Jay.

"The suit, right?" he asked.

"Wrong," chimed the saleslady. "The shoes are the statement piece."

"She's right," I said. Now we had to find a cheaper suit.

Once we found a cheaper suit, we needed a shirt. A nice one. Jay asked me if he should get a slim or a regular. I don't know the difference between a slim and a regular.

"Is it too tight in the shoulders?" he asked.

"Why does it matter if it's under the suit?" I responded. It had been two hours. My feet were starting to hurt and the tightness of a white shirt on Jay's arms under a jacket didn't feel important anymore.

When we finally had everything at the register, the saleslady didn't have the right shirt. She needed to run to the back and get it. Now my feet were really starting to hurt. I looked at my phone. It had been three hours since we got here, four hours since we left the apartment. That's my limit when it comes to shopping, standing, doing anything on my day off.

After what felt like twenty minutes, the saleslady returned with the right shirt.

"Do you have a Bloomingdale's card?" she asked.

"No," I said, holding out Jay's credit card to tell her I knew the spiel and the answer was still no.

"Oh, you should definitely get one. I can set you up with one real quick," she said, not picking up on my cues.

"No, I have enough credit cards. Thank you."

"Oh, but it's not a credit card. It's only a loyalty card. We'd just need your phone number and email and—"

"No thank you! Can you please just check us out so we can be done here?"

The man folding shirts to my left looked over, but I didn't care. The tension rising, the saleswoman put the loyalty card down and went back to ringing everything up. Only now she realized she didn't have the pants in the size we wanted, so she'd have to order them. "I'm going to have to get your shipping details," she informed us.

I watched her starting to type again with one finger. Our street name had twelve letters in it. "Are you kidding? How long is this going take?!" I yelled, forgetting who I was and where I was. She was sweating. But I didn't care how old and sweet she was anymore.

"We're almost done," she said reassuringly. I could feel Jay giving me that look telling me to calm down. But then she realized she'd ordered the shoes in the wrong size.

The shoes were the last part. But she'd rung them up wrong and now it was all getting shipped to our apartment and I was trying to tell her that she'd put our apartment down as 1B, not 1V. "Yes, that's V as in Victor," I told her, clenching my teeth.

"Okay," she said, really sweating now, "let me just start over. What's the address again?"

"That's it, I'm out of here. Fuck the suit! I can't fucking do this," I yelled, and walked out of Bloomingdale's into the sweltering heat of Midtown. Jay and I took the two trains home, not talking, sans suit, five hours of the weekend wasted. I'd embarrassed myself, again. If Anaïs Nin was right and it's in the moments of emotional crisis that human beings reveal themselves most accurately, then my true self was terrible. I'd tried to do something for someone else and couldn't follow through without a meltdown or a freak-out. I'd ruined a perfectly good Saturday because I couldn't control my temper. Now I realize it's because I didn't control my depletion levels.

Ever since that day, I've decided to start saying no when I think something will deplete me or if I know I can't do something because I'm already at a point of depletion. Well, not always no, but "another time." Because I'm tired of ruining the moments of life when I'm depleted. I've come to believe that emotional maturity means understanding my limits. Saying no when I need to. Skipping things that aren't going to fill me up. Knowing when I need to be alone and when I need others. I could have avoided the Bloomingdale's fiasco had I just listened to myself, read my own battery, and stayed home. Or, if I didn't realize I was depleted when I left the house, I could have excused myself when I felt myself deflating, told Jay I'd meet him at the café or the jewelry department, and quietly refueled.

BUILD INDULGENT RITUALS

One of the secrets of a happy life is continuous
small treats. —Iris Murdoch, *The Sea, the Sea*

There are moments in life when you can't just say no, unfortunately. Some Saturdays will be filled with errands and tasks, and like with my Bloomingdale's trip, you can't always foresee when you'll be depleted. Things like helping your kids with their homework after a long day at the office. Finishing that fifteen-page report your boss threw on you last minute. Going to your mother-in-law's for Christmas. In cases like these, when you can't stay home or turn your phone off, you have to get through with as much self-restraint and willpower as possible. But how? How does one exert self-restraint when it's run out?

Psychologists conducted numerous studies on how we can replenish self-control when we don't have the time to let it refill through rest and relaxation. The quickest and easiest way to recharge my battery was something I thought I knew how to do but was actually terrible at: treating myself.

In Elizabeth Gilbert's memoir *Eat, Pray, Love*, she talks about the importance of rituals as a way to put down negative emotions, to process the moments we pick up throughout the day and leave them there. "This is what rituals are for," she says. "We do spiritual ceremonies as human beings in order to create a safe resting place for our most complicated feelings of joy or trauma, so that we don't have to haul those feelings around with us forever, weighing us down."

Rituals are small, mundane things you allow in your routine that give you moments of peace and renewal. Things like taking a walk during your lunch break. Treating yourself to a manicure. Buying a new book for your subway commute. Running a bath on Sunday night.

What drains you and what refills you? What are those things that make you happy? What puts you in a good mood when the day seems to be headed toward meltdown? I think we've all forgotten how to stop and treat ourselves in small, caring ways. We're so used to the state of stress and depletion that we're actually uncomfortable out of it. Yet if we had more moments of pleasure throughout the day, we'd have more strength to deal with the annoying, painful ones.

According to recent studies, positive mood or emotion can counteract ego depletion. It sounds simple, but think about how hard it is to get yourself into a good mood when you're in a bad one. That's the catch-22 of ego depletion: You're stressed and agitated because your willpower is depleted, yet the only way to increase your willpower is through positive emotion, which you don't have the willpower to harness. That's when treating yourself becomes imperative.

In a study, participants did a task requiring self-regulation, then either watched a comedy show, received a gift, or did nothing. They were then judged on how well they performed another task requiring self-regulation. Those who watched the comedy video or received a gift performed better than participants who did nothing in between tasks. In fact, they self-regulated the next task as well as nondepleted participants (participants who didn't have to do the first task at all).

Taking the time to indulge in moments of pleasure is not selfish, it's restorative. In fact, knowing what can help put you in a good mood when you're headed for a meltdown or knowing how to pace yourself through the week so you don't experience burnout is a sign of maturity.

At thirty-four, Susan Sontag was a master list keeper who believed things did not have value unless she signified her interest in them. "Nothing exists unless I maintain it (by my interest, or my *potential* interest)." Her belief that things should be noted in order to exist led to her obscure and relatable lists of likes and dislikes.

Susan Sontag's Diary Entry (February 21, 1977)

Things I like: fires, Venice, tequila, sunsets, babies, silent films, heights, coarse salt, top hats, large long-haired dogs, ship models, cinnamon, goose down quilts, pocket watches, the smell of newly mown grass, linen, Bach, Louis XIII furniture, sushi, microscopes, large rooms, ups, boots, drinking water, maple sugar candy.

Things I dislike: sleeping in an apartment alone, cold weather, couples, football games, swimming, anchovies, mustaches, cats, umbrellas, being photographed, the taste of licorice, washing my hair (or having it washed), wearing a wristwatch, giving a lecture, cigars, writing letters, taking showers, Robert Frost, German food.

In Gretchen Rubin's book *The Happiness Project*, she focuses an entire chapter on splurges and happiness. In it she says, "What makes me happy is to spend money on the things *I* value—and it takes self-knowledge and discipline to discover what *I* really want, instead of parroting the desires of other people." She goes on to say, "If money is to enhance your happiness, it must be used to support aspects of life that themselves bring happiness to *you*."

So what made me happy? What tiny rituals could I add to my routine and indulge in more? For Susan Sontag it was coffee. For Gertrude Stein it was literature. For Carrie Bradshaw it was shoes. I found mine in a bottle of Bvlgari's Eau Parfumée. It was a free sample bottle I took from a hotel where Jay and I once stayed. This tiny vessel of liquid, when opened, transported me to another time and place. A place where I wasn't working or stressing or in my apartment that needed to be cleaned, but somewhere beautiful. Somewhere like Paris or Rome, where the light was soft and men with white gloves opened doors. Something about the scent in that little bottle refueled me, and whenever I felt weak or disillusioned, I found myself walking into the bathroom to dab some on the base of my wrist and behind my ears. It was so silly and so simple, but being surrounded by this scent as I continued with my day renewed me in a small, important way.

Cooking also became a ritual for me. Maybe it's because I was working from home and had more time, or maybe because I needed a place to put my nervous energy, but I became drawn to the rewarding pastime of creating and mixing and stirring things into form. Over time it became, inadvertently, my ritual. One of the few moments throughout the day when I found my mind at peace—not thinking about anything but the task at hand. I decided to let that be the place that I dropped everything. The time of day I allowed myself to let go of the things I *had* to do and refill on something I *wanted* to do.

Other rituals could be as simple and gratifying as lighting a candle every evening. The small act of lighting a match, the symbolic nature of burning, is grand enough to be a ceremony in the temple of your life. A place for you to burn away the day. Or maybe it's a cup of tea every evening. The drum of the kettle, the whistle, the collision of hot air. This can be your ritual. The moment the tea touches your lips is the moment you release it all.

After many years, I found more of mine: a new film at my favorite movie theater, Japanese pens from Muji, an extra-dirty martini, walks around Brooklyn at sunset, a piece of dark chocolate, a new book. These small, sometimes private ways to get back into a good mood when the day seems to be headed toward meltdown are the things that make you unique. They are your joie de vivre.

Rituals of Famous Women

Lee Radziwill

"I have an absurd kind of extravagance. If I see an orchid that's fantastically expensive, I'll buy it. It's worth it, for no other reason than it gives me pleasure."

Audrey Hepburn

"She had chocolate after dinner, baking chocolate. She had a finger or two of Scotch at night." —Robert Wolders, Audrey Hepburn's partner

Georgia O'Keeffe

"I like to get up when the dawn comes. The dogs start talking to me and I like to make a fire and maybe some tea and then sit in bed and watch the sun come up. The morning is the best time, there are no people around. My pleasant disposition likes the world with nobody in it."

Joan Didion

"I need an hour alone before dinner, with a drink."

Coco Chanel

"I only drink Champagne on two occasions, when I am in love and when I am not."

Elizabeth Taylor

"I love going to rock concerts...I love to lose myself in that vast wave of rhythm and body heat and get on the same vibe."

If you're having trouble coming up with small, healthy ways to treat yourself, I've outlined a few simple ways you can easily lift your day.

USE YOUR LUNCH HOUR

I always felt guilty taking lunch at work—like if I didn't run to Chipotle and eat my meal back at my desk within twenty minutes, I was a bad employee. I was taking advantage. I was walking on the edge. Now I see how ridiculous I was. No one was counting. No one was looking. *No one cared.* I was a good employee and got my work done. What difference did it make if I took the full half hour and ate my lunch outside?

RESCHEDULE YOUR PICK-ME-UPS

There are two things I'll never forget about an old coworker of mine, Melanie. The first is that she used to live with four girls in a loft in Chelsea. One night the roommates staged a house meeting to confront her. "You have sex too loud!" they told her. "Sophie had to stand on the balcony in the rain last night because you were so loud!"

Melanie told me the story the next day at work through tears. "I just don't understand why she just couldn't turn on the TV. Now it's my fault she got pneumonia because she stood barefoot in the rain?" she wailed.

The second thing I remember is that Melanie would always leave work after telling me a story like this to get a manicure down the block. She'd come back to the office forty-five minutes later, chipper, asking if we liked her newest color. I remember thinking what a waste it was—of both time and money. I thought of all the practical things she could do with that fifteen dollars. Today, however, I see her fifteen-dollar splurge as a small price for sanity. Her manicure was her safe haven, a way to replenish herself from the emotional turmoil of the city, her roommates, and her job.

You don't have to wait until Saturday to treat yourself. In fact, any dietitian will tell you it's better to have small treats throughout the week than to starve yourself only to relapse at McDonald's. Stop saving all these pleasurable moments for the weekend. The weekend is already good enough. What we all need are better Tuesdays and Wednesdays.

FIND A BETTER WAY TO WAIT

I knew that sleep and positive mood restored my pools of will-power. But what about things that could help keep willpower from depleting? If my willpower was a battery, were there things I could replace in my life that didn't need batteries?

Joyce Meyer wrote, "Patience isn't the ability to wait, but the ability to keep a good attitude while waiting." I was not a patient person. The subway delays. The holding time to speak with a service representative at AmEx. The lines at the bank. It all required too much self-control, empty time draining my will-power so I didn't have any left when I needed it. And then I found the *New Yorker*. Every week it arrived in my mailbox like a treat from the universe. It was my travel companion, my blanket, my binky. The ninety-nine-dollar annual subscription changed every line, every delay, every commute into a chance to read. Now, I could simply enjoy my *New Yorker* instead of exerting willpower practicing patience.

If you're not into reading, pay for a subscription to NPR, or the extra storage on your iPhone so you can download those full episodes of *Grey's Anatomy*, or just your favorite songs. Trust me, it's going to pay for itself twofold when it keeps you from that next meltdown.

REMOVE EXCESS CHOICE

> I find it easier to abstain than do a little bit of everything. I'm not a "little bit" kind of dame. I want it all, whatever I do.
>
> —Elaine Stritch

A few weeks after the blowup in Bloomingdale's I found myself feeling better. Or rather, being better for longer. Treating myself was easy to do and I loved finding new ways to indulge. But then, out of nowhere, I hit a wall. It had been a long day and I was in the middle of a bath when I received a text from Jay.

What do you want for dinner?

I don't care, you pick. I thought I was being generous but I also didn't have the energy to choose.

I can't think of anything. That's why I texted you.

Oh wow, I thought, *Jay's clearly in a mood.* I knew it would help the situation to just give him an answer but I didn't know what I wanted. And I didn't want to pick something we'd both end up not enjoying, then feel guilty for wasting money on overpriced takeout. I knew he didn't want to pick for the same reason. He thought I was picky. I started getting flustered. This was a sore spot for us. I'd seen these types of scenes play out in movies and TV shows, but never understood it before now. The reason couples fight over something as trivial as deciding on what to eat for dinner isn't about the food, but about who is going to exert the mental task of choosing the food. Choice, I realized, was another trigger of depletion.

Dr. Anne Thorndike, a physician at Massachusetts General Hospital, understood the power of choice and wanted to see if she could use it to improve the eating habits of hospital staff and visitors without changing their willpower or motivation. Noticing the unhealthy amount of sodas purchased throughout the day, she sought to change their decisions without changing their mindsets.

Thorndike designed a six-month study to alter the "choice architecture" of the hospital cafeteria, rearranging the placement of food and beverages. One change was the addition of water bottles to the soda-only fridge near the cash register. She also added baskets of water around the cafeteria food stations. In three months, soda sales dropped by 11.4 percent and water bottle sales increased by 25.8 percent.

Thorndike's study provided insight into the rationale behind the human decision-making process, confirming that we are influenced as much by where products are placed as we are by the products themselves. We don't necessarily want to eat the cookie, but we will eat it if it's there. One reason that we're not drinking more water is because we're not seeing water cues around us.

We make hundreds of choices throughout the day, so when your mind can, it will avoid making a choice. Rather than thinking about whether you should go back and get water because it's healthier than the soda, you grab the soda because it's right there and you'd rather not go through the decision process and extra effort.

Choices are the biggest drain of our willpower. They require us to think, to reason, to respond and make a decision. *Are you going to work or calling in sick? What are you wearing this morning? What are you packing for lunch? Or are you buying lunch? Or should you save money? Are you going to the gym or skipping it? Are you talking back or keeping quiet?* These small decisions all require willpower, and throughout the day our brain becomes like that poor Little Engine That Could—only at a certain point it *just can't*. It shuts down in those areas that control our good behaviors, our rational thought, our emotion control—our hippocampus.

According to John Tierney of the *New York Times*, "decision fatigue helps explain why ordinarily sensible people get angry at colleagues and families, splurge on clothes, buy junk food at the supermarket and can't resist the dealer's offer to rustproof their new car. No matter how rational and high-minded you try to be, you can't make decision after decision without paying a biological price."

Broadway star and Emmy winner Elaine Stritch struggled with the power of choice when it came to drinking. "You're scared, you drink, you're not scared" was her reasoning behind so many years relying on alcohol. It gave her confidence to stand in front of packed audiences and on-set cameras. It was her friend, her ally, and eventually, her problem. She'd been using it for the duration of her career and it wasn't until she was at a fabulous party in Paris at the height of her success, surrounded by celebrities she admired, that she had a breakdown. Some awakening after one too many gin martinis prompted her to quit the booze and get it together.

Well, not exactly quit. She promised herself she'd only have two drinks a day. One to give her the courage she needed to get up onstage and one to get her through it.

"Two drinks a day. Two drinks a day. TWO DRINKS A DAY! It doesn't work! Not when you want eleven, and not when you start shopping for wineglasses in the vase department at Bloomingdale's," she professed in her Emmy-winning one-woman show *At Liberty*. She had failed, and it was only after she'd had eleven drinks at a Woody Allen wrap party that she experienced a life-threatening diabetic episode that prompted her to quit again—this time without the two drinks a day. For twenty years Elaine remained sober, going to AA and enjoying a successful career without alcohol well into her eighties.

While I don't claim to know the science and psychology behind addiction and alcoholism, I do know that when it comes to quitting something, it's a lot easier to abstain completely than to have a little and stop yourself. It's a lot easier to have no fries than just one. It's a lot easier to have no wine than "just one sip." It's a lot easier to ignore your vices when you don't see them.

The only way to keep up your willpower and your energy throughout the day is to cut out unnecessary choices the same way you avoid unnecessary engagements.

According to James Clear, author of *Atomic Habits*, "It's easier to avoid temptation than resist it." It's going to be hard not to drink wine on Monday night when you see the wine bottle on the counter as you walk through the front door, depleted and tired. It's the elephant in the room—you can't not think about it now. Either you don't have the willpower to fight the urge or you'll use up the remaining willpower you do have and skip the wine but then skimp on that healthy dinner or giving the kids a bath. So why add that extra choice? Why not hide the bottle on Sunday night so you don't have to make the difficult decision not to drink on Monday? Controlling your willpower comes down to eliminating the number of choices you make on a daily basis.

Eliminating choices was a surprisingly liberating experience. I looked at choices like unwanted wedding guests. Which ones weren't worth it? Which choices were necessary and which didn't serve me? What could I stop dreading, pondering, stressing over? For a month, Jay and I removed all the alcohol from our apartment just to see if we could come home without having a drink. Without booze in the house, it became surprisingly easy. When we were desperate for a drink, one of us would have to go out and buy a bottle, which neither of us felt like doing.

When it came to those exhausting, fight-provoking choices like picking dinner, we decided on three go-to restaurants we both enjoyed that we agreed we'd have no qualms eating any night of the week. Once we made that decision, when it came time for one of us to choose the takeout, it was simply a matter of deciding if we were in the mood for Greek, Indian, or Thai. Three choices was less daunting and exhausting than the hundreds that appeared on Seamless.

The last thing I removed was something that had been depleting me for years. I didn't realize it until I started taking inventory of all the things that took up space in my mind and noticed how much energy I was spending on the daily task of worrying. Worry, I noticed, was a choice. I had to choose to worry about something my boss or my mom said. I had to choose to think about that thing I said or did. I had to choose to worry about how I replied to an email and if I should worry about what their reply meant back. I could worry or I could choose not to. I could just let it go and decide not to even think about it, which inherently meant I just chose to always let things slide more.

CHANGE THE WORDING

> Your word is your wand. The words you speak
> create your own destiny.
> —Florence Scovel Shinn, *Writings of*
> *Florence Scovel Shinn*

I remember realizing just how many acts of willpower it took to get me to work, through work, and home after work. All those acts created the impossible mood I found myself in upon returning home. Once I started treating myself, adding rituals to my routine, and removing things I didn't want to use willpower on, I found myself able to get through the workweek with twice the amount of energy and half the number of breakdowns.

There was one thing, however, I still hadn't mastered. One thing that had nothing to do with work at all, but rather the idea of work: Sunday Scaries.

If depletion is what creates the mood after work, Sunday Scaries are what create the mood before it. I was spending Sundays curled up on the couch watching mindless TV to numb the anxious voice in my head. I was sick of being snappy and distant with Jay because I was distracted by all the problems that *could* go wrong next week. I wanted my Sunday to feel like my Saturday. And why shouldn't it? I had two days off; why could I only appreciate one of them?

Then, like so many buried memories of the past, I recalled a moment that seemingly had no significance at the time and now illuminated with the present with meaning. It was an especially dark Sunday a few years earlier, and a few months before the demise of my relationship with Roxanne. After three years in the city together, Roxanne and I had gone from living together, to meeting up a few times a week, to only seeing each other on the weekends.

We were still close, but we were changing and evolving into new versions of our adult selves at such a rapid pace that sometimes I barely recognized her. The distance between our apartments had widened over the years and the bridge between my Brooklyn neighborhood and her Manhattan one seemed to symbolize the new distance between us.

When we did get together, we had less in common, less to talk about. Our history and our memories were the thin thread that kept our relationship together and the fragility of it was palpable. I didn't want to admit it to myself, but I wasn't sure if I even liked Roxanne anymore.

She was still fun and warm and had that energy I loved about her, but with that energy there was a darkness. She was sleeping with men who I didn't want to be around. And she was staying up all night and sleeping all day and her apartment was littered with vodka bottles and past-due notices and remnants of a life I didn't want for her or myself anymore.

I yearned for the Sundays we had spent in Central Park together, drinking wine, splurging on cheese, basking in our new life in a new city, too happy and full and distracted to think about Monday.

How many times had I woken up hungover in Roxanne's bed and just feel...depressed? What was I doing here? Why was her apartment so dirty? Who was that guy on her couch? I'd sink back into her bed and pull the covers over my eyes. I couldn't spend Sunday like this. I needed to feel safe and secure. I needed to be in the light, not in this dark cave. I needed to stop wasting my Saturdays doing things I couldn't remember on Sunday.

"Jesus Christ, Lauren. Nothing's wrong. You're just hungover!" Roxanne would scream at me when I woke her up saying we needed to get our act together, that I was seriously freaking out.

Nothing's wrong, you're just hungover. The phrase reverberated in my ears as I walked down the brownstone's crumbling steps toward the Union Square subway. It was so simple yet so effective. I wasn't depressed. Nothing was wrong. I was just dehydrated, tired, hungover.

Our friendship didn't last, but the idea Roxanne planted in my head did. I found myself repeating that phrase to myself whenever I woke up miserable or anxious after a night out. The pain of my hangover was a cue to remind myself that my perception of the world around me was skewed because of my weakened state of mind, not because anything had changed.

During this particularly difficult bout of Sunday Scaries, I wondered if I could apply that same technique—to use the nerves of Sunday to remind myself that nothing was actually wrong, but just butterflies about the week ahead. "Calm down. Nothing's wrong, it's just Sunday," I told myself.

But it didn't work. The feeling still sat there. My motivation was gone and I resigned myself to another day spent watching reruns of *The Real World: Cancun*.

As it turned out, I could use a phrase to alter my emotional reaction to Sunday Scaries. I just needed to choose different words. A few weeks later I was lamenting to my therapist about how nervous I was about an upcoming trip I had to take for work. "Are you nervous?" she asked. "Or are you excited."

"Nervous," I responded.

"What if you simply told yourself you were excited?

"What if," she continued, "you tricked your brain into thinking those butterflies in your stomach were good butterflies?"

"Ok," I said. "I'm not nervous. I'm excited." Upon saying it I instantly felt better. The knot in my stomach didn't feel as tight and the idea of traveling didn't seem as terrible. Anxiety reappraisal, she explained, is a cognitive trick based on the concept that words can trigger emotions. Like songs or smells, words have memories and associations attached to them. The word *excited* arouses a different emotion than the word *anxious*. I had anxiety about Sundays because I was calling them scary. In order to change the way I felt, I could start by changing the language I was using to describe how I felt.

So when I was sitting on the couch on Sunday, stewing over the week ahead, worrying about all the emails and that thing my boss said to me at Friday's happy hour, I was thinking about how anxious I was while simultaneously telling myself to calm down.

What many of us try to do is replace anxiety with the concept of calm. This doesn't work because calm is not an aroused emotion. Excitement, like anxiety, arouses emotion. It increases heart rate and cortisol, preparing our body and mind for action. But excitement produces a positive emotion, unlike the negative one anxiety produces.

According to Alison Wood Brooks, a professor at Harvard Business School, it takes a lot more effort for us to go from a negative state of arousal to a state of calm than it does for us to go from a negative state to a positive state of arousal. Moody women understand this. It's easier to go from happy to sad (or sad to happy) then it is to go from any emotion to "chill." We're not "chillers."

To illustrate this concept, Brooks performed a series of experiments. In one of them, she asked participants to sing Journey's "Don't Stop Believin'" in front of the group. The participants were told to say either "I'm excited," "I'm anxious," or nothing at all before they broke into song. According to computerized measurements of volume and pitch, the "excited" group actually sang better. When asked to give two-minute speeches, the same result happened. The "excited" group spoke longer, and were seen as more persuasive, confident, and persistent.

A similar study was done in the realm of ego depletion by marketing professors Juliano Laran and Chris Janiszewski to understand self-control and the effects of depletion on behavior. They found that the way we perceive work-related tasks correlates to how depleted we feel. When we think a task is going to be fun, not only will we spend more time on it, but we will feel less depleted by it.

> **Replace "Calm down" with "I'm excited."**
> **Replace "I don't want to" with "I get to."**
> **Replace "I'm scared" with "I'm pumped."**

Besides just eliminating the number of choices I made throughout the day, I discovered that I could actually shift the way I thought about the choices I couldn't avoid. I could stop dreading the things I had to do and start reminding myself that I get to do them. Because activities were only depleting if I thought they were and stressful situations were only scary if I thought of them that way. Monday was only scary if I thought about it being scary.

How you go through your life is shaped by how you think about things. The mind is as strong as it is weak, and we can use its susceptibility to our advantage. We can trick ourselves into thinking that increased heart rate, sweaty hands, and the pulse of adrenaline aren't anxiety but excitement. Like magic, we can also deceive ourselves out of a depleted state with rituals and tricks. The opposite of work is play, and if we can learn to add more play into our lives, to stop taking every email, obstacle, and problem so seriously, we may just be at the cornerstone of chill.

THE MOOD TRANSFORMED

Caring for myself is not self-indulgence, it is self-preservation.

—Audre Lorde, *A Burst of Light*

The unendurable is the beginning of the curve of joy.

—Djuna Barnes, *Nightwood*

I do, I undo, I redo.

—Louise Bourgeois

THE MOOD:

FRIENDS

Symptoms include: isolation, paranoia, and an unhealthy obsession with "read" receipts.

THE MOOD DESCRIBED

What I craved at this point was not love, or romance, or a life added to mine, but conversation, which was harder to find.

—Mavis Gallant, "Varieties of Exile"

Needing people yet being afraid of them is wearing me out.

—Janice Galloway, *The Trick Is to Keep Breathing*

Oh, sometimes I think it is of no use to make friends. They only go out of your life after awhile and leave a hurt that is worse than the emptiness before they came.

—Lucy Maud Montgomery, *Anne of Avonlea*

I'd been waiting for it for weeks. When it arrived one Saturday morning, I was alone and didn't immediately rush to get it because I was in sweatpants and hadn't washed my hair, and it didn't feel like the right way to accept this sort of package. An hour later I sauntered down the hall, into the building's brightly lit foyer, and asked Thomas at the front desk for it. It was big and heavy, and carrying it back to my apartment I had that nervous, elated feeling one has before a blind date.

I placed it on the large gray marble countertop and found scissors to break the tape. Inside the box was another one, an expensive-looking navy box. I unwrapped the white bow around it, took off the lid, and pulled out a garment bag. Attached to the garment bag was an envelope. Trying to draw out the experience, I opened it the same way children open their stockings before the presents under the tree. Inside the envelope was a small white card with pink cursive lettering: *Congratulations on your beautiful custom wedding gown. Instructions for use:*

1. Remove all makeup before trying on.
2. Make sure you have a friend with you to help with those hard-to-reach buttons.

I stared at the card until the letters became indistinguishable, the words morphing into symbols. Then I took the garment bag out of the box and walked it to my closet, hanging it up at the far end next to my unworn dresses and stained sweaters, refusing to unzip it. I didn't want to see it. I thought I'd be sick if I saw it. I hated it. It didn't matter what it looked like, I wanted it out of my sight.

I hadn't thought about this. That when I got the dress I'd need someone to zip it up. I guess I had thought about it unconsciously, when I designed it online instead of going to a store with friends and family like every other bride. I should have known there was no way I could have this wedding and not confront this mood. Because it didn't start with the card. The card was the trigger, but the mood had been bubbling under the surface for years now. Maybe since middle school. Maybe since high school. But definitely since Roxanne. Or rather, since the end of Roxanne. After eight years together, our friendship ended with two text messages that were so juvenile, so unsophisticated, that when I think of them I feel sick. Yet as childish as those words seem, we'd had fights before, said cruel things we always took back later, they'd lain there for three years, neither of us having the courage to replace them with new ones.

Don't ever talk to me again.

Don't worry I won't.

Until that warm, dense summer morning when the dress arrived, I'd felt fine about it all. I had my fiancé, my coworkers, my family, my peripheral friends. I reminded myself how many nights I had wanted this. How many nights living with Roxanne in our first apartment on the Upper East Side I had wished for this solitude. Like when I'd come home and the lights would be off and I'd pour myself a glass of wine and look at the TV in the living room and wish I could grab a blanket and curl up on the couch, get comfortable, really comfortable, but instead I'd retreat to my windowless room, close the door, the air stifled and suffocating, and watch something in the dark on my laptop. Because she'd always come back. I'd hear the drunk jangle of her keys, fumbling their way into the hole, or her heels on the cracked linoleum as she barged in with some guy or coworker, and even though I'd be in a robe or sweatpants, I'd feel exposed.

I had what I'd been longing for. The boyfriend, the apartment, the engagement; it all happened so effortlessly. I had what so many others wanted. Only now, three years later, I wanted what everyone else had. I wanted what felt like a prerequisite to being female—the brunches, the dinners, the group chats. Yet every time I went out and tried to find it, it all felt forced. Or fake. And I'd come home with a pit in my stomach, overanalyzing every word, every text, every silence. And the more I went out, the more I tried, the more I felt like an outsider.

I thought my life was going to be different than this. I thought my wedding would be filled with bridesmaids and a maid of honor and groups of friends from different pasts. Instead, it felt like this wedding was a symbol of an irreparable failure I'd made in my life. It was a sign that I was unlovable. Unfriendable.

I no longer had the confidence in myself that I'd had when I was younger. Like a woman after a bad breakup, I was paranoid and insecure. After the last fight with Roxanne, I'd let go of our mutual friends, assuming that because she'd known them longer or better they'd naturally side with her. And all my other friend-ships, the ones from high school or Spain or camp or work, felt like limp ropes in my hand that, no matter how hard I pulled, wouldn't tighten.

Over the past three years I'd become judgmental, irritable,

and disillusioned. I'd thought the older I got the more social I'd become, but the opposite was happening. I was lonely. And the loneliness was palpable. I felt it all the time. I felt mocked by it— on television, walking to work, passing girls having breakfast at a corner café. The worst part was that I was ashamed. Because at almost thirty, I shouldn't be searching for friends. Now was when others were solidifying their friendships by becoming godparents and maids of honor. It felt like I had missed the boat. I had placed all my chips on Roxanne and lost.

In that moment I was glad Jay was traveling for work. Glad that I had the apartment to myself to wallow in. I needed room to mourn, space to tunnel further into myself. I spent the night stalking Roxanne's Instagram, binge-watching *Grace and Frankie*, and ignoring the one text I did get. I wasn't in the mood to grab a drink with a former colleague, I was in the mood to isolate myself and feel completely alone.

WHAT THE MOOD IS TELLING YOU

I tried to blame the mood on Roxanne. Then New York. Then my job. I told myself I liked solitude. That I didn't have time for friends. But the reality of the statement contradicted my feelings, which were that every Instagram post of former friends felt like a punch to the gut. Every unreceived invitation felt like a personal attack. The further I withdrew, the more days I spent in a state of self-loathing or anger after scrolling through Facebook.

But I couldn't withdraw any longer. My wedding was forcing

me out of the cocoon I'd built for myself and into reality. It was a crash course in the mood I'd been avoiding for years. A looming finish line that I would either cross or break down before ever reaching. Every step of it was a trigger. When I had to pick flowers for the bouquet, I thought about how I'd have no one to hand them to. When I looked for shoes, I thought about how there'd be no one to strap them on for me. When I stared at Pinterest looking for a hairstyle, I remembered I had no one's opinion to ask.

Just a few weeks after the dress arrived, my family threw a surprise bridal shower for me. My mother knew I didn't want one, so it was small and informal and rather than traditional wedding gifts, she asked people to bring their favorite book. After it was over and I had gotten drunk and cried over how few friends of mine were there, I spent the next morning opening the pile of wrapped books on my parents' dining room table. One of these books had a deep pink cover with white lettering—*Toward a New Psychology of Women*. Because I was always looking for interesting content for Words of Women, I took that one to my room to read. When I started reading it, I didn't find anything for Words of Women; instead, I found an answer to the pain that had pervaded my life for the past few weeks.

The author, Dr. Jean Baker Miller, a psychiatrist and psychoanalyst who provided groundbreaking insights into female relationships, proposed that **women's sense of self revolves around being able to make and maintain relationships**. And that for many women the disruption of these connections is perceived not just as a loss of a relationship but as something closer to a total loss of self.

That one explanation summed up how I was feeling. Lost.

Disjointed. Unfulfilled. Like I was missing some vital part. Like I was constantly on the verge of completely alienating myself and never being allowed back in. I didn't need the book to know that the female identity was shaped by friendships. That women need tight bonds to feel safe and supported. What I needed a book on was what happens when you don't feel like you have those friendships. What happens when the friend you once thought you'd spend your life with gets married, has kids, moves away, and becomes nothing more than an acquaintance? What happens when the friends you make in high school, the ones you'd promised to be friends with forever, change, and no matter how many times you get dinner, the differences are too palpable to stomach? What happens when your work wife stops calling after taking another job, leaving you to stalk her on Instagram, wondering if it was ever real to begin with?

According to Miller, these changes in friendships, these losses, hurt. They hurt the same way a breakup or a burned hand hurts. That social rejection is processed as physical pain. When we feel rejected or snubbed, even by a stranger, our brain triggers the same neural circuits that process physical injury. Due to old evolutionary patterns that once relied on human connection for safety, the threat of social disconnection triggers an automated fight-or-flight response, and even though our sociological structures have changed, that response hasn't. Further research has also found that as children, if we're rejected when we reach out, that rejection is stored in our amygdala, the part of our brain that processes emotions, and we grow up associating the desire for connection with rejection.

Moments like this leave fragments within us. Compounded by years of betrayals, ghosting, and rejection, we develop skewed perceptions about the world around us. When we see a picture of our friends hanging out, or get a text message that we can't understand, we process it with a negative, often false, interpretation. We assume they are hanging out without us because they don't like us. They didn't invite us. They don't want to be our friends anymore. We think the text is rude or weird and they're trying to tell us something they don't have the courage to say directly. We believe our own false narrative so much that we act as if it's really happening. We cut them off before they can cut us off. We stop texting them. We isolate ourselves, and in turn create the reality we so feared.

I'd been acting on these negative perceptions for years. After Roxanne, I did it with the few friends I had left. I assumed every picture one of our mutual friends (which we had a lot of, since we met in college) posted with her was directed at me, rejecting me, making their choice clear. I projected my hurt from her onto them. I stopped texting them for fear they wouldn't text back. I stopped liking pictures for fear they wouldn't like mine. And finally, I didn't invite them to the wedding for fear they wouldn't RSVP. In not inviting them, I brought to life the false narrative I was so afraid of. I acted upon some thought that wasn't real, but my actions made it real.

In psychology, this specific self-fulfilling prophecy is known as the acceptance prophecy. This phenomenon shows that if people expect acceptance, they will act warmly, which in turn leads people to accept them. If people expect rejection, they will behave coldly, which will lead to less acceptance. We build our own realities through our beliefs and will those beliefs into reality through our actions.

But real life isn't like psychological experiments. We're not given feedback as to whether or not someone likes us. We make those determinations based on clues. And most of our clues are projections of our self-worth. Negative self-worth creates negative projections—for example, my reaction to the small white card. All the anxiety and shame and fear I felt was based on my own insecurities, but I was projecting it onto everything around me. Everything hurt. Everything felt like an attack. Everything was negative because I was negative.

This small white card was my trigger and awakening. Because even though I said I didn't want this wedding, unconsciously I did. I had created this moment because I needed the jolt. If I could override the negative perceptions I'd built, if I could change my habits and projections, I could save myself from this mood and the isolation it brought. And once I changed how I felt about myself, I changed how I saw things. Once I changed my perceptions, my life opened up in a way I never expected.

FIND YOUR FLOW

> The most important relationship in life is the
> one you have with yourself.
> —Diane von Furstenberg

Emotional distress, according to Dr. Miller, is always the result of disconnection, be it disconnection from other people, the self, or a larger community. I felt like I was disconnected from all three and it seemed like the best way back would be to start with myself. Because somewhere along the line, whether it was in the last three or thirteen years, I'd stopped being comfortable with myself and, in turn, my relationships. I'd become so insecure, so isolated, I didn't know where I stood with anyone, let alone myself. I realized the question wasn't *What kind of friends do I want?* The question was *What kind of friend am I?*

I thought I was a good friend. I could be fun. I was always on time and respectful and tried not to cancel plans. But I knew I was drinking more. And I was irritable. And judgmental. And I gossiped sometimes. Okay, a lot. And I never understood why I did it. Like that time at that bar in the West Village. I was with an old high school acquaintance who'd messaged me out of the blue to see if I wanted to grab a drink. After two white wines, we started talking to the two guys next to us and soon realized we had an acquaintance in common. Specifically, I knew someone the taller, blonder guy knew. Another writer. A writer whose book I'd read and enjoyed. Yet when he asked me what I thought of her book, I dismissed it. "It wasn't that great," I said.

"Oh, I thought it did very well," he said.

"Maybe for her," I said, regretting it the moment the words left my mouth.

As a result, I spent the next two weeks asking Jay if he thought the other writer would find out about what I said. "I wouldn't worry about it," he said. "But why'd you say it?" Because I'm insecure. Because I don't think I'm a good writer so I have to project my fears of failure onto others. Because I have no control over myself.

I told him I didn't know. But I knew that I didn't want to be this person. I also knew that my chances of becoming friends with her were now that much slimmer. I'd sabotaged the friendship before it began while also showing those guys, and my high school friend, a side of myself I didn't like.

I was projecting my insecurities onto those around me, pretending I couldn't accept people, when in reality I couldn't accept myself. "The more we love ourselves," Louise Hay said, "the less we project our pain onto the world." Unknowingly, I was projecting an energy that came from a deep place of pain. Carrying my insecurities around like armor, I was no longer comfortable, natural, easy to be around. I knew I wasn't as fun as I used to be, like I was in high school and college. Whenever I went out it felt like I was straining to enjoy myself, like reality, the party, the real fun was in some parallel universe and I needed four or five drinks to get there. I needed alcohol to get comfortable, to start to feel like my old self, to break down the walls between myself and everyone else.

I wasn't fun to be around, and in turn, others weren't fun around me. I was stuck in a loop. I was in pain because I felt excluded, so I projected a negative energy, and that energy was reflected back to me, which I interpreted, feeling more excluded. The energy we release into the world is the energy that returns back to us. I knew that was true. I knew because when I left my apartment one of two things occurred—the world was with me or against me. There were those magical New York days when the city vibrated, every person on every crosswalk and in every bar was a new friend to be met, a stranger with a story, and I remembered why I came to this city, the city with eight million people, for this, this energy. And then there were those days when New York was the enemy. When my doorman gave me a weird look and the strangers were rude and the people in the bars were cold. But the city doesn't wake up in a bad mood. Eight million people don't just decide one day to be nice and another to be mean. The city was a reflection of me.

Vanessa Van Edwards, a behavioral investigator who spent years conducting studies on people's emotions and behaviors, found that humans catch emotions. And the emotions we catch from someone make us either like that person or dislike them. **And the reactions of those people create the energy we feel around us.** According to Van Edwards, "Whether we like to admit it or not, we decide if we like someone, if we trust someone, and if we want a relationship with someone within the first few seconds of meeting them."

Take how Jay always gets in a bad mood because I'm in a bad mood. Edwards found that our microexpressions, which include real smiles, fake smiles, looks of fear, stress, and anxiety, induce the same feelings in others. Even when we think we're doing a good job hiding our feelings, these subtle facial expressions give us away. It's why a certain tone in my mom's voice when she answers the phone puts me on edge. Or why I get paranoid when I notice a change in my boss's face. Or why even when I came home and tried to pretend to be in a good mood, Jay could always tell.

It's impossible to be happy all the time, however. No one should ever aim for that goal. Instead, we should aim to love ourselves all the time. Because unlike happiness, self-love isn't fleeting, yet like happiness, it attracts and emanates good energy. Corny as it sounds, self-love is really just less self-judgment. Less overanalyzing, less negative self-talk. In Buddhist terms, it's known as *maitri*. One of the four Buddhist virtues, the word translates to "friendship" or "friendliness." If one learns to develop *maitri* they have learned self-acceptance and can flow through the world in a state of equanimity. According to Buddhist monk Pema Chödrön, "The only reason we don't open our hearts and minds to other people is that they trigger confusion in us that we don't feel brave enough or sane enough to deal with. To the degree that we look clearly and compassionately at ourselves, we feel confident and fearless about looking into someone else's eyes."

So many of us have difficulty with self-love because our automatic thoughts override it. Automatic thoughts are the immediate thoughts that occur after negative events. Many times, our automatic thoughts are distorted. These distorted thoughts happen so rapidly, we barely notice them, let alone take the time to question them. Yet it's these thoughts that create our moods. Every event is really just our thoughts about the event. If we can learn to think differently, to change our automatic thoughts, we can change not just the way we see the world around us but the way we move through it.

---

5 Pathways to Distorted Thoughts

Assuming: Little evidence leads to broad conclusions.

Your boss looks like she's in a bad mood, so you automatically assume it's because you did something wrong.

Shoulds: Differences create comparisons.

Your friend is funny; you should be funny too.

Overgeneralizing: Isolated events create sweeping descriptions.

Because you stopped being friends with someone, no one will be your friend again.

Personalizing: Things that have nothing to do with you are all about you.

Because your daughter dropped out of college, it's a reflection on you as a parent.

Making Feelings Facts: How you feel is how things are.

You feel anxious, and there must be a reason for this. You must have done something wrong.

Being aware of these distorted thoughts was the first step in correcting them. I could train myself to look out for them, to realize when a thought was following one of these patterns and change the narrative. Of course, I didn't go from years of judging myself to loving myself overnight, but every time I corrected a distorted thought, I felt myself growing. The real change, however, in my energy, my flow, didn't happen until I learned how to replace the distorted thought with something I had never thought to give myself before—love. I hadn't realized that I had to practice self-love just as intensely as I practiced any other new habit. Like most of the lessons in my life, I learned how to do this from a stranger in spandex.

I guess I wouldn't call him a stranger. He was the vinyasa

yoga instructor at Equinox. We had been doing downward dog for what felt like fifteen minutes, my arms were sore and starting to shake, and I was scanning the room to see if anyone had retreated to child's pose when his voice came out of the dark. A soft, gentle voice commanding us to "Hold the pain. Find your sweet spot." After transitioning to a more accommodating pose, he went on to tell us a story about a previous class he was teaching when he noticed a student having a hard time. He could tell she was frustrated and disengaging from the class, so he stopped her on her way out to find out if anything was wrong. She told him that she'd had a rough week at work and that she came here to try to relax, but not being able to do the poses made her even more stressed. He told us the reason she, and so many of us, have such a hard time in yoga is not because we're new or not flexible, but because of the way we talk to ourselves.

Through the years we have developed a habit of talking to ourselves negatively when we can't do something. We're mean to ourselves, aggressive even, and this negativity seeps not just out of us, but through us, inhibiting us from reaching our full potential. It's the reason we can't do the poses or go further in our practice. We talk ourselves out of being able to do it and then judge ourselves for it.

He asked us to practice talking to ourselves differently this class. When we couldn't do something (touch our toes, hold the pose, etc.), instead of admonishing ourselves, to he wanted us to find our *sweet spot*—a moment of compassion and self-love. Your sweet spot, he explained, is when you acknowledge where you are and what you're against and you ask yourself to go just a little bit further, to hold the pain just a little bit longer. Instead of getting worked up or angry when we felt our arms giving out or our legs shaking, we acknowledged the beauty of what our body was doing and with gratitude asked it to do just a little bit more. And it was in the gratitude and the love we showed ourselves that we found that extra kernel of energy, that extra strength. This change in how we talk to ourselves, encourage ourselves, enabled *flow*.

Outside of yoga, sweet spots are those moments when you want to judge yourself, when you want to monitor yourself, but instead you give in to yourself. Like that time when I was nervous before a conference call. My boss would be on it and I was expected to talk to the client. I always hated these types of calls. Should I be funny? Should I be serious? Instead, I thought about my sweet spot and decided to be myself—to accept whatever naturally came to me. To give my opinions without judging them. To talk without overthinking what I was saying. To respect myself for being on the call, at the job, and honor my abilities. Nothing felt different, except that the anxiety, the weight, the stress was gone. And after the call my boss texted me, *Great job!* Then she did something she never does, tried to make chitchat. She asked about my wedding, my dress, my date. I responded without overthinking and ended the day realizing that when I was myself, I didn't worry about gaining approval because the approval was already there.

REJECTION ISN'T REJECTION

We are afraid to care too much, for fear that
the other person does not care at all.

—Eleanor Roosevelt

After the arrival of the card, I told myself I was going to start making more of an effort. I told myself that while I might not find another best friend, I could still develop the relationships I had on the sidelines. One of those relationships was with Lucy, a friend I'd lost touch with after high school but occasionally saw because we both lived in New York. I'd gone to her birthday party in Crown Heights even though it was a thirty-dollar Uber ride, went to a play with her in Times Square, met her for a drink after work *in the rain* on two occasions, and since she'd moved to Nevada five months before, I even talked to her on the phone.

On one of these calls she had told me she would be able to come to my wedding. That it worked out because her cousin was having her baby the same week. I didn't ask whether she'd be coming if her cousin weren't having a baby. Then she told me she'd talked to Tedda, another high school friend of ours in New York. They were still close, while I hovered on the periphery with both of them. "How is she?" I asked.

"Good. She got promoted," she said.

"That's awesome!" I replied. "I should reach out and congratulate her."

I wanted to send Tedda a message, but since Lucy had moved, I hadn't kept in touch with Tedda as much. Though Tedda and I had a longer history together, our relationship fizzled when Lucy wasn't there to organize things. The last time I spoke to Tedda was probably three months prior, when she messaged me about getting together one night. We never ended up hanging out because she was busy traveling with work and never set a firm date. I hadn't reached out to set one because I figured she would be busy. It's not that I didn't want to see Tedda more; just the opposite, in fact. I felt I couldn't see her enough because she was always busy with other friends. Mignon McLaughlin has a quote that perfectly describes the type of person Tedda is: "Every now and then you run across radiantly attractive people and you're delighted to find they adore you, till you realize that they adore just about everybody—and that's what's made them radiantly attractive."

Tedda was one of those people with lots of friends. Gaggles of college friends and camp friends and work friends. Friends with lake houses and mountain houses and beach houses. It felt like trying to maintain a friendship with her was fruitless. She already had her friends, I wouldn't be able to get the time I needed from her. It was easier to just see her when Lucy was in town. Which was why, just a few weeks after getting off the phone with Lucy, I felt like I'd been sucker punched after stumbling over an Instagram photo of the two of them drinking Aperol spritzes at a bar down the road from my apartment.

Why hadn't Lucy told me she was coming to New York? Why hadn't she invited me out with her and Tedda? I had just invited them both to my wedding but wasn't close enough to have a drink with them? The pain moved through me like a wave. I walked into the living room, where Jay was sitting on the couch playing video games, his eyes glued to the screen as I talked.

"Tedda and Lucy were hanging out last night," I said like someone reporting an unsettling piece of company information to upper management.

"Oh yeah? Did they invite you?"

"No." I turned and walked back into the bedroom, hoping to exude an attitude of boredom or apathy so as not to invite further conversation about it. Because the tears had escaped and I didn't want to admit to Jay, or myself, that I was crying like a middle schooler over friends who didn't invite her to sit with them at lunch. With the bedroom door closed and Jay blissfully unaware of the whirlwind of torment and pain spewing out of me, I proceeded to ascend through the stages of rejection, similar to those of grief.

First there's disbelief.

Maybe that wasn't Brooklyn. Maybe they're in some weird town in Nevada. Maybe that wasn't Lucy. Maybe that was an old photo she's just reposting.

Then self-pity.

So it's true, they don't like me. Lucy comes back to New York for a night and I'm not invited. The two of them made plans without me because I'm disgusting and annoying and abrasive and will never have friends.

Then rage.

What the fuck is wrong with them? I've been trying to hang out with Tedda for months. We texted last week and she said she was traveling for work. Now I see she's in Brooklyn hanging out with Lucy? Why couldn't she just invite me? What the fuck did I do to her?

I had worked myself into a frenzy. "I am going to send a text," I said, walking back into the living room, Jay still staring at the screen, tapping buttons on a white Xbox controller.

"If that'll make you feel better, then do it," he said.

"I'm going to," I said, walking back into the bedroom and closing the door.

Hey Tedda, I don't want this to sound weird or alarm you but I was just wondering if something was wrong? Because I feel like I've been trying to hang out with you for a few weeks now and it hurt me to see you were hanging out with Lucy the other night.

I stared at the drafted words, my thumb hovering over the send button, then put the phone down to think about it a bit more— to figure out whether the thoughts I had were reflections of reality or just automatic and distorted. I picked up my phone again and tried to see the situation as Tedda would if I sent the message. I scrolled up to the last conversation we'd had. Looking at it, I saw the situation from Tedda's eyes. She had been the one to initiate contact after a three-month lull. She had been the one to tell me she was traveling during the week but free on weekends. I was the one who never made a plan. I was the one who hadn't sent a text in three months. Why should I rely on Tedda to do all the work? I was the one who was expecting her to lead the conversation, the charge, the invitation. But she'd already done her part. I could follow up. I could have made a plan. But I didn't.

I didn't send the text. I didn't send it because it would make me look crazy. I had perceived the situation with a negative skew that wasn't accurate or reflective of Tedda's actual behavior. It re-minded me of the time I noted to Jay that our dog looked sad.

"He doesn't look sad, he's just resting," he said.

"No, he's definitely sad," I responded.

"Why would he be sad? He's just lying there, relaxing."

Jay and I were looking at the same thing, yet I was viewing it negatively. Studies on people suffering from depression found that they observed people's faces as sad or upset when they were neutral, a phenomenon known as negativity bias. I wasn't depressed, but I viewed things the same way. Only I judged people's actions as bad or evil when they were just neutral. I interpreted people's responses, messages, and behavior as hostile, when they were really just being themselves. If someone's not happy, they're sad. If they're not messaging, they're mad. If they're not inviting me, they're excluding me.

I thought of that Freya Stark quote: "One is so apt to think of people's affection as a fixed quantity, instead of a sort of moving sea with the tide always going out or coming in but still fundamentally there: and I believe this difficulty in making allowance for the tide is the reason for half the broken friendships."

It came down to expectation. I expected people to be a certain way. I expected friends to say and do the things I'd say and do for them. And when they didn't, I felt betrayed. If someone didn't respond in the right way, I assumed some evil reason and wrote them off. Or at least, I'd write them off until they made some appropriate move. But I wouldn't dare reach out. Until this time. This time, I decided, I was going to stop withdrawing and confront the situation.

Instead of sending the drafted text to Tedda, I sent a different one. I asked her if she was free in the coming week to grab a drink. She responded warmly and we set a date. There was no mention of Lucy, of inviting her or not, because it wasn't about Lucy. It was about the two of us. And once I started seeing that, how the plans I made were never a reflection on the people not in them, I stopped seeing every missed invitation and Instagram post as a rejection.

Then I learned more. When we met up for dinner a few weeks later, I decided to be bold one more time. After a few drinks, I told her that I saw she'd been out with Lucy a few weeks ago and that it hurt me a bit because I would have loved to see them both. "Oh my god!" she said. "I didn't even think about that." She went on to tell me that the two of them had never actually made plans, that the meetup was by chance. Tedda was at that bar with colleagues for a going-away party and Lucy happened to be there on a date with some fling she'd left in New York. "She actually got a little drunk and told me how lonely she's been," Tedda said.

A light spread through me. How wrong I had been. How absolutely, ridiculously wrong. Nothing was ever as it seemed, and if this Tedda and Lucy situation was any indication, I needed to start reevaluating every conclusion I made from here on out. I decided, then and there, that I would use every perceived rejection as a reminder to start reaching out more.

EVERYONE'S A FREAK

She recognized that that is how friendships begin: one person reveals a moment of strangeness, and the other person decides just to listen and not exploit it.

—Meg Wolitzer, *The Interestings*

In an odd but kind of makes-perfect-sense way, Joan Rivers and Prince Charles were good pals. Not inner-inner-circle, claims Rivers, but outer-inner-circle friends. And every Christmas, Prince Charles used to send Joan a gift. More than once, he sent her two fancy teacups. In typical Joan fashion, one year she sent a thank-you card with a picture of her standing in front of her Christmas tree with the two teacups and wrote, "How could you send me two teacups when I'm *alone?*" The next year she sent another thank-you note with a photo of the teacups. This time in a cemetery with the caption, "I'm enjoying tea with my best friend!"

After two years and two cards, she never heard anything about the thank-you notes. "He never acknowledges it! He never says to me when I see him, 'Ohhhhhh, funny funny funny!'" So she assumed she'd offended him and wrote her next thank-you note normal and polite with no teacup jokes or photos. Only after sending it, she ran into a mutual friend who told her he'd just been with Charles, who told him he could not wait to get Joan's note that year.

Why didn't Charles tell Joan he loved the notes? Maybe because he was embarrassed. Maybe because he's English royalty and repressed. Maybe because he's awkward. There were a million possible reasons why, but Joan could only see the reason as it pertained to her. And the queen of uncensored comedy censored herself.

How many times have I done that? How many times have I censored myself or backed down from what I wanted to say because I didn't feel I would get the right response? How many times have I misread silence for anger? How many times have I overthought something because someone didn't respond the way I expected? My pivotal moment, my learning curve, came just a few weeks later.

Hey Lauren! How's it going??

I'd been writing and didn't see the message. It was from an old college friend I hadn't spoken to in a few months. In fact, we spoke so little these days I wondered if we were considered friends anymore. She lived in Boston, so I only saw her on the rare occasion she'd be in town. Seeing it a few hours later, I felt like a kid who missed the dolphins jumping at the zoo. I immediately responded. *Hey! So sorry I missed your text. I'm good. How are you?* I sent another. *How's Boston?*

I felt that made up for it. Five hours later she responded: *It's great.* I waited for the three dots. For her to ask me a question, to tell me she was visiting, to give me the reason she texted me in the first place. After five minutes and no dots, I figured I'd prompt her once more. Maybe she was busy. So I replied: *That's awesome! How's everything else going?*

Three days went by and I still didn't know why she'd texted me because she never responded. And even though she had reached out to me, I felt rejected. I spent my weekend wondering if in the three hours between her texting me and me texting her back she had learned something awful about me and decided she didn't actually want to know how I was doing anymore. Or maybe she didn't mean to text me in the first place. Or maybe she wasn't as good of a friend as I thought she was. Or maybe, as Jay pointed out, she was just a freak.

Maybe she was just like Carlson, an old coworker who sent me a message after not talking to me for three years to congratulate me on my new job I'd started two years ago. And I said, *Thanks, Carlson! How have you been?* But he never responded because, well, he's also a freak.

Or Carly, who showed up to a rescheduled brunch twenty

minutes late after canceling on our first one. Carly, who made me feel like a second-tier friend because when she finally did respond, and we finally did hang out, she never cared enough to arrive on time. But really, she'd just have been having a fight with her parents—the parents she thinks don't love her, so she's now seeing a shrink at $200 an hour, and because the shrink is so expensive she has to ask her parents for money, which in turn makes her feel guilty and project that guilt onto her parents—during which time gets away from her and now she's twenty minutes late to brunch.

I used to think that Carlson not answering and Carly showing up late were signs that there was something wrong with me. I used to spend days obsessing over the things I could have said or did to make them act that way, when I could have just realized and accepted that maybe it had nothing to do with me at all. Maybe they were just as wrapped up with their own lives as I am with mine. And they'd forget to respond not because they hated me, but because—like I sometimes did too—they got busy and forgot or missed my message.

In one of those old Hollywood anecdotes, Debbie Reynolds relates a story about Bette Davis: "If she didn't want to talk to you on the phone, she'd pretend to be somebody else. Imagine! with that voice. 'Miss Davis is not here. Who's calling? Just a minute.' And she'd go away and she'd come back and say, 'Hello, Debbie dear. I wasn't sure I was here.'"

If I were friends with Bette Davis and she told me in her own voice that she was unavailable to talk and would make sure I got the message, I would spend the next two weeks in a state of anxious tension. *What does she mean she's unavailable? Why doesn't she want to talk to me? Why would she pretend not to be herself? Does she think I'm stupid? Was she trying to play a game with me?* And it would be Jay who'd have to pull me out of the spiral and note, in a perfectly rational and calm way, that Bette Davis is also just a freak.

We don't know what's going on in people's lives. Not really. We can think we know, and they may share one or two details, but we don't actually know. And we can't ever know what someone is dealing with silently. What flaws and stresses and preoccupations are overtaking them, causing them to act the way they do. Deborah Tannen, an expert on communication and relationships, says all of our conversations are products of our own personal histories. What we say and how we say it is all a personal style that we've developed after years of interacting with people. The way our family talks to us or shows love becomes the way we speak and show love. And this is what creates conflict. We think we understand what someone is saying, but we are only really hearing them through our own filters.

Only when we realize that our personal interpretation of someone's words and actions is usually inaccurate can we stop stressing so much about every interaction and start enjoying the people around us. If I could let things slide, if I could realize everyone is their own weird, eccentric, unique freak and just accept them as that, I'd feel less stressed and worried about what they think of me. And in stressing less about what they mean or think, I will project a better energy and develop stronger friendships.

We're All Freaks

Kay Thompson, author of the famous Eloise children's book series, came up with the idea because when she was nervous or bored she would talk in the voice of a four-year-old.

Tallulah Bankhead called everyone "dahling" because she was terrible at remembering names. One specific instance was when she introduced a friend of hers as Martini. Her name was Olive.

When someone asked Margaret Wise Brown what time it was, she'd respond, "What time would you like it to be?"

Whenever Carole Lombard would go away on location, she made sure that at least once during the production she would host a waffle party for the cast and crew using her waffle iron. When asked the secret ingredients that made her waffles so special, she would say cornmeal, lemon ricotta, and strawberry rhubarb compote, while, in actuality, her waffles contained none of these.

It's so freeing, so liberating, so energizing to put down my expectations of others and watch them come to me as they are. To have them surprise me and teach me and remind me that everyone is so uniquely and beautifully different. Simone Weil said that attention is the rarest form of generosity, but I'm starting to believe acceptance is the rarest form of generosity. Then again, maybe attention and acceptance are the same thing. *I see you* is the same as *I accept you*.

DOING THINGS YOU DON'T WANT TO DO

> To see takes time, like to have a friend
> takes time.
>
> —Georgia O'Keeffe

There is a caveat to being too chill—to letting everyone do what they do and talk when they want to talk. Because while I believe that life is best lived under the proclamation of *what will be will be*, I also know that friendships don't work if everyone takes that attitude. Friendships, unlike fate, need some attention.

I've never been good at giving attention. I was an accepter, not a reacher. A reacher is someone who extends invitations. Someone who makes the plans, sends the first message, asks how the other person is doing. I didn't do that. I accepted. I happily responded when someone reached out to me. I made an effort only once effort was made. This was because I'd gotten comfortable with solitude. Too comfortable. I wasn't just fine spending Saturday and Sunday alone, I was used to it, and after years of getting used to it, I'd become numb to it, then addicted to it. The more I barricaded myself in, the scarier the outside world seemed. The more I stayed home, the harder I found it to function in the real world. My social skills became rusty, and the less I used them, the harder they were to find them when I needed them.

The relationships I'd developed after Roxanne were mainly

with colleagues at work. They were built from commonalities— how much we hated our job, our boss, our other coworkers. After we'd spent eight hours a day together for six months, Frances asked me to hang out with her outside of work. We went to the first bar we found near the office. She couldn't go there because she was gluten free. "Oh, I didn't know that," I lamented.

"Yeah, well technically I'm not allergic, but I know I will be soon. Just cutting it out as a precaution."

"Oh," I said. "How about this place?" I asked.

She looked at the menu. "They don't have Corona. That's the only beer I can drink."

So we went to another bar. But it didn't feel like when Roxanne and I jumped from bar to bar looking for the right place. This was the opposite. This was looking for the right menu and ignoring all sense of ambience. We ended up at a fluorescently lit Mexican spot. I asked if she wanted to order tacos. She reminded me of her gluten allergy. An hour later, all out of office gossip and having expelled our work frustrations, we'd gotten to the point of finding new common ground. When I asked if she'd ever seen *The Crown*, she told me she didn't watch TV...or movies. She only watched *Friends* because it was the only show that didn't give her anxiety.

When I got home Jay asked me how it was. I told him about how she didn't like TV or movies.

"So what?" he asked.

"So, what are we going to talk about?" I asked.

"Other things," he said.

"I can't think of anything else," I told him.

"How about the fact that you also have anxiety?" He was joking when he said it, but thinking of it later, I realized that might have been something worth talking about. That would have created a strong bond between us, the sharing of two similar struggles. Instead, when I left that job, I left Frances. When I think back to the relationship, I feel a pang of regret. I was so quick to dismiss her. So quick to let that possible friendship go. Even though we got along so well at work, I figured since the conversation wasn't as natural outside of the office, it wasn't worth pursuing. I didn't realize that sometimes you need to put in effort when it doesn't come naturally. Sometimes you need to sit with someone for a while, show up a few times, until it starts to feel right. Sometimes friendships don't flow like a natural spring. Sometimes they need patience and time and days when you're doing things you don't want to do.

It all just felt too hard. Like if a friendship wasn't coming as naturally as it had with Roxanne, then it wasn't worth it. It wouldn't work. But what did Roxanne and I actually have in common? While we shared similar philosophies, weren't our differences bigger? In the end, wasn't it our differences that drove us apart? We were friends because of our history together, the memories we shared, the years that accumulated. Shouldn't my relationship with Roxanne be proof that time could create bonds between two different people?

A psychological theory known as the mere-exposure effect proves this point. The theory stipulates that people tend to like other people who are familiar to them. In one example of this phenomenon, psychologists at the University of Pittsburgh had four women pose as students in a psychology class. Each woman showed up in class a different number of times, never interacting with the male students. When the male students were shown pictures of the women, the men demonstrated a greater affinity for those they'd seen more often in class. We like people the more we see them. We trust people the more we get to know them. And that trust forms the basis of friendships.

Another study was done to see how long it took freshman students to make new friends. The researcher found it took:

- 50 hours of interaction to move from acquaintance to casual friend
- 90 hours to move from casual friend to friend
- more than 200 hours to qualify as a best friend

It comes down to putting yourself out there—again and again. Accepting that friendships don't happen overnight, but are the result of sticking it out, finding common ground, and getting to know someone when it's not always that natural or easy. Knowing that with enough effort and time, it'll become fun.

* * *

One month before the wedding, I scrolled past a photo of an old friend. Kayla, Roxanne, and I had all been good friends in college, but when I stopped talking to Roxanne I also stopped talking to Kayla. It wasn't because Kayla ever did or said anything, but because I assumed she was better friends with Roxanne and wouldn't want to be friends with me anymore. And the more pictures I saw of Kayla and Roxanne hanging out, the more I believed it. But after all this, all the months I'd spent analyzing the friendships I'd had and lost, all the misread cues and misinterpreted conversations, I realized Kayla might not have taken any side. Kayla and I might have stopped talking only because I was the one who stopped reaching out. Yes, she could have reached out too, but maybe she felt the same way I did. Maybe she thought I didn't want to be friends with her anymore. Maybe she thought *I* would think it was awkward. Maybe, I thought, this time I could be the brave one. So, holding my breath, I reached out with a text. And she responded right away. A week later I met her for a drink and apologized. I told her I'd spent the last few years believing all these lies I'd told myself and that's why I hadn't reached out. That's why I hadn't invited her to the wedding. Then I pulled out an invitation. I told her I understood if she couldn't make it since it was last-minute. But I wanted her to know that I did want her to be there and I did value our friendship. She wasn't able to make it because she already had a wedding that weekend. But the difference between who I am now and who I had been three years before was that now, I didn't take it personally. I didn't spend days in a funk, wondering if she wouldn't have come even if she didn't have plans. Wondering if she made up having another wedding to go to. Wondering if there was a jab under the excuse. I didn't see it as a rejection. I saw it clearly, and for the first time, for what it was. She was busy, and that had nothing to do with how she felt about me.

The last thing I did, two days before the wedding, was send a message to Roxanne. I was a little drunk after two beers in the train station, but I needed to break the silence. I needed to clear away the ugly stain of our last words.

Hey, I know we're not talking but I just wanted to say that I miss you. I know I have things to apologize for and I would do that here, but I think if any apology is to be done properly it should be in person. So if you ever want to grab a drink let me know.

She didn't respond and for the first time I can recall, I didn't worry about it. Then three days later, she did. She told me she missed me too and that yes, she would be willing to grab a drink sometime.

As of now, we still haven't gotten that drink. I still look out for her whenever I'm in her old neighborhood, still think every small blond woman bounding toward me could be her, still play back old memories like a favorite movie, but neither of us have followed up because deep down, though the door may have cracked open, we both know it'll never be like it was. What we had, like a romantic relationship, can never be the same. Roxanne and I stopped being friends because like so many friends, we grew into different people and when you add relationships, new jobs, new cities, new children, the gap between us became too wide. But now, at least with the text, the new words wiping away the stench of the last ones, we got a little bit of closure and we can let that chapter of our lives go. More importantly, I know that our relationship didn't rest on my inability to reach out. There were no questions, no afterthoughts, nothing to wonder about anymore. I could close that chapter and focus on making new friends.

THE MOOD TRANSFORMED

Sometimes you find that what is most personal is also what connects you most strongly with others.

—Grace Paley

I shiver. Thinking how easy it is to be totally wrong about people—to see one tiny part of them and confuse it for the whole.

—Lauren Oliver, *Before I Fall*

The point is to reach out honestly—that's the whole point.

—Anne Sexton

THE MOOD:

FAMILY

Symptoms include: feelings of judgment, rage, disappointment, and tantrums over turkey.

THE MOOD DESCRIBED

One situation—maybe one alone—could drive
me to murder: family life, togetherness.
—Patricia Highsmith

We did not fight. Nothing was wrong. And
yet some nameless anxiety colored the emotional charges between me and the place that
I came from.
—Joan Didion, *Slouching Towards Bethlehem*

But I think that sometimes, when one's be-
haved like a rather second-rate person, the
way I did at breakfast, then in a kind of self-
destructive shock one goes and does something
really second-rate. Almost as if to prove it.
—Alison Lurie, *Real People*

It was Christmas, a few months after the wedding. After the photos had been printed and hung on the wall and thank-you cards had been delivered and I had been away from my family long enough to feel that small twinge of excitement about seeing everyone again. On the ninety-minute ride from New York to Philadelphia I'd pumped myself up enough to believe that this year would be different. I was older, more mature, and aware of the triggers that provoked me. There would be no outbursts, no fights, and no complaints. This Christmas, I thought, would not be like every other Christmas.

I forgot that going home was like going up a mountain. The air thinner, the mind weaker, and the senses heightened. I forgot about all the history, mistakes, and undertones that crunched beneath my feet. I forgot how hard it was to acclimate.

This time started off well enough, however. I made it through Christmas Eve—the dinner party, the church service, the car rides. Christmas morning, Christmas lunch, then right when I thought I was safe, that I'd be on the train the next morning with three clean days under my belt, I lost it.

It was around four o'clock, the sun already setting, the drinks already flowing, and Michael Bublé's Christmas album wafting from the speakers when the front door flew open in a gust of icy wind, sending a chill up my spine. Aunt Linda had just arrived, carrying her traditional Christmas cookies and steaming plate of judgment.

It's not that I don't like Aunt Linda. I am conflicted about her in the way you're conflicted about the mean girl in high school who's being nice to you. The youngest of my dad's four sisters, she has a confidence that came from years as a cheerleader, then a sorority girl, then a country club member. A suburban mom of two kids, she still exudes the aura of a cool girl, with that way of making you feel comfortable with gossip and wine and that electric attention of hers, until you drop your guard, and right when you're not looking she jabs you.

After arriving, her husband hanging up her coat, my mom taking the tray of cookies in her hand, and my sister pouring her a glass of wine, she made her way over to me. We began by reminiscing about my wedding. We then talked about future plans, jobs, apartments. Eventually she brought up the drama in the house she'd just come from. My cousin's house. I asked what it was about and she told me that ever since my cousin got married a week ago, there had been tension. My cousin had been a mean bride on the day of her wedding and made her mother cry. Her mother, Aunt Linda's older sister, was too weak to confront her daughter, so Aunt Linda did. She told her she had acted like such an ungrateful brat all through the wedding and now she was ruining Christmas. I expressed shock and laughter when appropriate and eventually said something like, "Wow. That's crazy. What's wrong with her?" to which Aunt Linda replied, "Well, you should know. I heard you were a bitchy bride."

It was just a comment. A passing comment. No one else heard it, yet my ears were ringing, my head was fuzzy, and I was bleeding out on the floor. I'd been shot. Not in the heart, in the gut. Not by a pistol but by a shotgun, the type of gun that leaves a big, round, gaping hole. Did anyone see that? The ice in my glass clinked as I brought it up to my lips. "Um. Who told you that?" I asked, knowing it could only be one person.

Noting the pale color my mom had turned behind me, Aunt Linda began backpedaling. "Oh no, I was thinking of my other niece," but the damage was done. The mood was bleeding out, soaking through me the way the glass of red wine I spilled in ninth grade soaked through my parents' white couch.

I felt a surge of rage and shame, two tributaries intertwining and merging together into a river at the bottom of my heart. The same feeling as when my brother used to sock me in the stomach or someone slammed into me on the soccer field. *Is this how my mother sees me? Is that how I am to her? A bitchy bride? Just because I cried one time in the hotel room because the makeup artist never showed up? Did that make me a bitchy bride? And did my mom have to tell Aunt Linda that?*

I turned to my mother. "Why would you say something like that to Aunt Linda? Why are you talking about me?"

Her face still pale, mouth slightly open, she had the look of a woman ripped out of a warm chardonnay buzz. She told me she never said that, then my aunt said that all brides are bitchy. The back-and-forth continued until my mother eventually said, "You did have that one moment," at which point I exploded. I wanted to cry, but I wouldn't break down in front of them. Instead, I yelled. I told my mom I was never coming home for Christmas again. I told my aunt that she was a nosy bitch. I told my mom that the reason I was so bitchy was because she made me stressed. She was neurotic and psychotic and I would never talk to her about anything again.

Then I drank three more gin and tonics, ignored my aunt for the rest of the evening, and cried to Jay in the bedroom. I was pissed with myself. Pissed that I was pissed. Pissed that even though it'd been years since I started this project, I still couldn't control my moods around my family. It was like all the progress I'd made in the real world dissipated the moment I walked back into theirs. I was supposed to be getting better, not unraveling at the first jab from Aunt Linda. If Aunt Linda was a test of my success as an emotionally mature, self-assured, confident woman, then I had failed. But why? What was it about my family that had the power to provoke this mood?

WHAT THE MOOD IS TELLING YOU

We are like sculptors, constantly carving out of others the image we long for, need, love or desire, often against reality, against their benefit, and always, in the end, a disappointment because it does not fit them.

—Anaïs Nin

Of all people, it was my father who blew this mood open for me. The next morning, sitting in the passenger seat of his car on the way to the train station, I couldn't stop myself from bringing it up. "Can you believe what Aunt Linda said to me?" I moaned. I knew he was the wrong audience to go to for pity, not only because Linda was his sister, but because he was a man.

"Oh, that's just Linda," he said. "She's always like that."

"Always like what? Mean? Rude?"

"Oh, she's not that bad. That's just how she is. What were you expecting?"

"I mean, that my aunt would be nice to me."

"She is nice to you. She's like that with everyone. The only difference is you expect something different from her. Whereas everyone else is used to it."

"I just don't think I'll ever get used to someone like that," I said.

"Well, you'd better get used to it, because she's not changing."

There it was. The reminder, yet again, that I was trying to change a trigger rather than adapt to it. Only this time I was trying to change a person. I expected her to behave one way, then felt blindsided when she didn't. I assumed that because I'd never say something like that to her, she would never say something like that to me. I put all these expectations on her and when she didn't fulfill them, I was pissed. All this anger, all this hurt, this entire mood was really just disappointment.

According to psychologists, anger is often used as a response to disappointment. An easier emotion to convey than sadness or shame, we cover our disappointment with being mad. As philosopher Martha Nussbaum believes, "We are prone to anger to the extent that we feel insecure or lacking control with respect to the aspect of our goals that has been assailed—and to the extent that we expect or desire control. Anger aims at restoring lost control and often achieves at least an illusion of it."

The entire mood I felt around my family was wrapped in anger. Anger when they didn't respond the way I wanted them to. Anger when I called to tell them I got a promotion and instead of congratulating me they said things like, "Did you get it in writing?" Anger when my mom didn't communicate with me the way other moms did. "I hate you" is always really just code for "I'm disappointed," isn't it?

This mood wasn't anyone's problem but my own. Through the years, due to movies and my own hyperactive imagination, I'd built up these roles of how people were supposed to act. I'd developed this code of what a good family, a good friend, a good husband should do, and whenever anyone deviated from that script, I reacted. But what if I tore up the script? I felt a twinge of liberation at the thought. It would be so easy to let it all drop. To let the curtain fall. For the first time in twenty-eight years I shook off all the preconceived ideas, notions, and history of those near me and decided to look at everyone with fresh eyes. The cure to this mood would be to accept people as they were, instead of how I wanted them to be. Of course, that would have to start with understanding the roles I'd put everyone in, including my own.

REALIZE EVERYONE'S ROLE

> People...do not change, they are merely revealed.
>
> —Anne Enright, *The Gathering*

Before I could accept everyone else, I had to take a hard look at myself. Was I acting out in a certain pattern? What expectations had I placed on myself as daughter, sister, wife?

Therapist Virginia Satir spent her career studying the relationships between family members. She believed every family casts its members into roles, and these roles, no matter how damaging and inaccurate we know they are, are ingrained within our family dynamics.

Our roles are communication styles—ways we've learned and grown accustomed to interacting with our family. They keep everything running in a certain "harmony," and every time you talk to your mom or sister, they expect you to take on this role. Because if you act out of character, they're forced to improvise—and nobody likes improvisation unless they're paying for a class at UCB.

According to Satir, there are five styles of communication that families are likely to adopt. Rather than acting authentically, each family member reverts to one of these five roles and communicates based on the values and habits of that specific role.

Blamers: "I am both worse and better than you thought."
—Sylvia Plath

The sensitive and spirited ones of the family, blamers are the first at our side when we need them and the first to jump down our throats if they feel betrayed, slighted, or disrespected. Highly attuned to imbalances, they're the dutiful daughters, mothers, and sisters who try their best but can't stop showing their worst when something feels wrong or unfair. Even though they're sweet people, they have an aggressive reputation for lashing out when hurt.

Distractors: "If my life wasn't funny it would just be true, and that is unacceptable." —Carrie Fisher

Distractors are the jokers of the family. The ones who would rather deflect than engage. They're quick to steer the conversation away from anything that verges on "too deep" or "sensitive," using humor to overcompensate for things they'd rather not feel. Distractors are great for easing tension but can be volatile if forced to get serious.

Computers: "If anything, I turn away; into greater and greater detachment." —Martha Gellhorn

Computer communicators refuse to explore that deep emotional place, and in an effort to protect themselves, they intellectualize the situation. When angry or hurt, they use reason as a defense. Clinging to rationality and fact, they hide the pain of their emotions behind logic, refusing to drop their guard and meet others on a human level.

Placaters: "I didn't know who the hell I was. I was whoever they wanted me to be." —Natalie Wood

Placaters are the neutral ones who deny their own feelings and needs by obsessing over everyone else's. The ones in the family always trying to keep everyone happy and from fighting. By doing this, however, they not only delay the underlying tensions from breaking but also suppress their own emotions.

Levelers: "I'm not offended by all the dumb blonde jokes because I know I'm not dumb...and I also know that I'm not blonde." —Dolly Parton

If there's a golden child, it's the leveler. This is the type of communication style we should all aim for. Levelers are emotionally mature individuals who are not afraid to express their own vulnerabilities for the sake of peace or progress. They are direct without being combative. They are emotional without being emotionally charged. They engage in ways that are authentic and not layered in double meanings or feelings. They are open and receptive to criticism and honest communication. They make others feel comfortable, heard, and understood.

It was obvious that I held the role of blamer in my family. When my mom asked why I hadn't told her about the speeding ticket I got my junior year of high school, I told her it was because she would freak out. When she brought up my "bitchy moment" at the wedding, I told her it was because she stressed me out. I made the situation about her, rather than admitting my own failure or mistake. This automatic response was because I had developed this aversion to disappointment. Like all blamers, I would rather lash out than be seen as anything less than perfect. My entire role was built around avoiding and deflecting so as not to ever feel the pain of disappointing.

It was the same reaction I'd have when confronted by Jay. When he'd ask me why I hadn't called to let him know I'd be late, I told him it wasn't my fault he was needy. These impulsive reactions all stemmed from this role I'd adopted. Once I understood the role I kept reverting to, I was more conscious when I felt myself entering it. I could also see the roles others were taking and would try to communicate with them on a level that engaged with them rather than enraged them.

I saw all these roles play out like an off-Broadway play just a few months later when everyone was back home for my grandmother's ninetieth birthday. We were in a dimly lit steak restaurant and I'd just ordered my second gin and tonic when my sister made some offhand remark about the time I got a dog in college and had to give it to my parents when I couldn't take care of it. There was absolutely no question about her role; she was, and always will be a computer—because everything she says is always based in "fact," even if the fact is something no one wants to talk about. I felt attacked, stripped naked in front of the table. How dare she expose me like that? Though she wasn't saying anything my parents didn't already know—they still had the dog and loved the dog—I felt like I'd disappointed them all over again. I lashed back, pointing out that at least I'd finished college. That maybe she wouldn't notice the dog if she weren't living back at home. At which point my dad jumped in, making a joke about how he loved the dog and my sister because they were both bitches, and that's when I spotted it. The roles, so clear, so distinctly defined in front of me.

I'd seen this before: different setting, exact same play. I knew what would happen if I continued to respond to my sister—it would be like that last family vacation, when she had made a comment and I lobbed one back and my dad chimed in but we ignored him and I continued to fight until my father, calm distractor though he was, exploded in a fit and left the table. At which point my mother, the placater, tried to calm us all down before going to the bathroom to cry about how her children could never get along.

Seeing the roles, I could rewrite the ending so it wouldn't conclude the way it always did. There was no use responding to my sister; she would only argue back with more digs and facts. Instead, I could use my dad's joking as a warning sign. His role was my cue to stop engaging and let it go for the sake of peace. There was also liberation in understanding my sister's role. You can't fight with a computer, and at nineteen, she wasn't going to mature anytime soon. The one thing I could do was accept her as she was, or even better, find compassion for her under all the cold facts she was spewing out.

When you understand your own motives, impulses, and triggers, you can better adapt to the motives of those around you. Understanding I was a blamer made me rethink why I always had to respond. And understanding that my sister was a computer made me less triggered by her responses. When I understood everyone's roles, when I could see them as clearly as my own, I could focus on changing the way I communicated with them.

COMMUNICATION VERSUS CONVERSATION

I'm always interested in how people use language to not say what they mean.

—Greta Gerwig

So much of my expectation, so much of this mood, lay in how I was trying to connect with those around me—what I wanted them to say, what I expected them to say, and what they actually said.

In the early 1900s, fashion icon Diana Vreeland wrote in her diary, "Mother and I agree on practically nothing...I cried this morning. I feel like crying now. I don't know what to do. It really isn't fair toward mother. If only I knew what to do. I do nothing but argue and contradict mother and it must stop. It's awful but I can't help it. It's one of the big problems of my life today. I can't tell mother. I would not know what to tell her."

It soothed me to know that women of different centuries had woes similar to mine. Knowing the late editor-in-chief of *Vogue* once felt the same pain and insecurity about her relationship with her family made me feel less isolated about mine. Like Mrs. Vreeland, I felt like there was a wall of things that my family never talked about. All these memories and uncomfortable moments we experienced but never digested or put to rest. And it became clear I wasn't going to move past the mood until I dug them up, wiped them off, and put them back down in a new place, one that wasn't roped off with caution tape.

One of the most shameful moments I had never properly processed and put to rest, was from years past when I was studying abroad in Madrid and my mom, sister, Aunt Gabbi, and cousin came to visit me.

A few weeks before they arrived I had met someone. I had been studying at an outdoor café when a man and a woman approached me. "Perdona," the man said. "Can we borrow this chair?" He switched to English upon seeing my face, I knew it. I had the opposite of a Spanish look—my overly highlighted hair and Juicy sweatpants were a dead giveaway to my American status. But I was feeling cheeky and answered back in Spanish. My answer, or maybe my tone, my eagerness, delighted him and instead of taking a chair, he asked a new question. "Can we join you?"

His name was Roberto and he was a forty-year-old dentist who lived in the La Latina (imagine East Village) neighborhood of Madrid. The attractive blond woman was his French tutor.

Or so he told me. The conversation quickly became flirtatious and when the French tutor got up to use the bathroom, he got my number.

A few nights later we met for a date. He was less attractive than I remembered. His black hair was greasy and thin, spiked with gel in a way that only suits younger men. He had a few lines on his forehead and his teeth were overly bleached, but he also had a confidence I wasn't used to, at least not in American men. (Not that I would know. I had gone from single in high school to miserably single in college and this was my first stint in the "real world" of dating.) He told me I looked like Hannah Montana and even though I was insulted, I went back to his place with him. After two weeks of sleeping over at his black marble bachelor pad, I believed Roberto was my boyfriend.

I, Lauren Martin, age twenty-one, was sleeping with a man twice my age. Not just a man, a dentist, who had his own place and a 2011 Range Rover. And although he whistled at girls in bars and had never driven me to school, even when he knew I was running late and the subway would be crowded and take longer than the normal forty minutes, he was mine.

So when my family arrived, my mom and aunt having postflight cocktails in the hotel lounge, my cousin and sister drinking Shirley Temples, I was excited to tell them about my "relationship."

When my aunt finally asked how everything was, I replied, "Great! I'm seeing this amazing guy."

"Oh yeah? Is he another student?" she asked.

"No. He's a dentist."

I watched my mom and aunt exchange looks.

"How old is he?" It was the first question my mom asked.

"Forty," I replied, with confidence.

I watched them exchange more looks.

"Well, that's great. Maybe we'll get to meet him." Aunt Gabbi was always supportive.

My mom didn't say a word and *that feeling* started bubbling up. That one I always felt around her. Like nothing was ever good enough. Nothing was ever right. Nothing was ever easy. She'd just arrived in Spain, hadn't seen me in three months, and couldn't even pretend to be interested.

"How are classes?" she finally asked.

"Fine. Normal."

"Shall we go explore, then?" my aunt asked as my cousin started sucking on the ice from her Shirley Temple. The group went to their rooms to change and I stayed in the lobby texting Roberto.

As we walked out the revolving door of the hotel, my aunt held me back. "Your mom wants to make sure you're on birth control," she whispered.

"Of course I am! Besides, it doesn't matter. This is a serious relationship."

I wanted to sound strong, but I was hurt. Why was all she cared about whether I was being safe? The question felt less like one of concern and more like one accusation. Another reminder that she was the parent and I was still the immature child. I was living alone in a foreign country, speaking another language, legally old enough to drink, and she still made me feel like I had no idea what I was doing. How come she didn't want to ask anything about Roberto, but did want to gossip behind my back to my aunt about something as awkward and uncomfortable as birth control? Couldn't she talk to me about it herself?

To me, this side comment was an indication that even though I was twenty-one, my mother and I weren't going to be friends anytime soon. She wasn't someone I could confide in or feel comfortable sharing things with. It still felt like any time I had good news, she made me question it. And like the roles I didn't understand at the time, I was now reverting to the one that always got me in trouble.

After an afternoon of sightseeing, we headed to El Mercado, my new favorite dinner spot, the one Roberto had taken me to on our first date. And coincidentally, the same one Roberto was taking another girl to that night.

When I saw him, holding hands with her across the table like in every Debra Messing film I'd ever seen, an anvil fell through my heart to my stomach. I couldn't breathe. There he was. At the same table he'd shared with me, across from a girl who looked just like me. I was staring at him long enough that he eventually looked up. But when we locked eyes, I turned away. I was going to be sick. I was such an idiot.

I was too proud to let on to my aunt, let alone my mom, that my "relationship" was what everyone knew it was: a creepy older Spanish guy just looking to give the *jamón* to a young, naïve American girl. So I sat there, seething, writhing, repressing the hurt.

And what does someone repressing hurt, anger, and embarrassment do? She drinks. But I didn't want to drink alone in the streets of Madrid, so I decided to bring my fifteen-year-old cousin Nina with me, got *her* drunk on tequila shots, and returned her throwing up at two a.m. to my aunt's hotel room. Then I went to my room, shared by my mother and sister, and attempted a strip tease (don't ask me why, it was a phase in college that started and ended that night). And like always, woke up at four a.m. with that painful jolt of consciousness—*what had I done?*

Later that morning, I was sick. Not physically, emotionally. I would have been physically ill, but the distress of it all had my stomach in knots. *What happened? Why is there a trash can next to my bed? Why am I naked?*

It was around nine a.m. and I was alone in the room collecting my thoughts when my sister came in from the lobby.

"Where is everyone?" I asked.

"Eating breakfast."

My stomach tightened.

"What happened last night?"

"You were naked and dancing and mom made me shut my eyes!" She started laughing.

Oh God.

"What happened to Nina?"

"She was sick this morning so Aunt Gabbi told her to stay in bed."

Oh God.

"Is Mom mad?"

I knew the answer.

"Yep!"

She laughed, leaving the room.

This wasn't going to be easy. Not only was my mom pissed at me, but my cool aunt was most likely upset with me too. I got her fifteen-year-old daughter drunk, and who knows what I had said to any of them while I was myself completely intoxicated. When I finally met them for breakfast I started apologizing before I even sat down. I told my aunt I would do anything to make it up to her. I told my mom I was sorry about everything.

I told them both I'd behave myself the rest of the time they were there.

I didn't tell them about Roberto. I didn't tell them that I drank because I was too embarrassed to admit what really happened with my "serious relationship." I didn't tell my mom that I left dinner hurt not just about Roberto but also about the birth control comment and the fact that we weren't close enough to have that conversation without a middleman. I didn't tell either of them that I felt uncomfortable, sad, and lonely in this foreign country.

My mom didn't say anything except "You should apologize to your aunt again." So that was that. We flew to Barcelona the next day, and the rain on the double-decker bus tour, where we sat on top, felt like an omen. Everything went on as usual, but nothing felt right.

As a writer I should be able to transition this story, tie it up in a nice bow, seamlessly integrate how it relates to the anxiety we feel around our family, but I think I just needed to get the eight years of shame and embarrassment off my chest. I've been carrying it around because I never could resolve it, bury it, end it on my terms.

Because last year at Christmas, when Aunt Gabbi had a few drinks and asked Jay if he'd heard about the "Spain story," I cringed and tried to change the subject. I couldn't laugh about it with her because I was still ashamed of it. Clearly she had gotten over it; she was laughing about it. But I wouldn't join in because even as a joke, it reminded me that she still remembered it had happened. And if she remembered, then my mom definitely still did. But why was something I did at twenty-one still bothering me? Why couldn't I let this part of my past go?

Because I never confronted it. And you can't get closure on something you refuse to face.

I've learned these small (or big) moments in our family don't just "go away." They have to be faced or else they only deepen the wedge. It's natural to make mistakes, to embarrass yourself around the people you love, to go through stages and periods of growth that look like destruction. It's not natural to never be able to talk about it. But that's why families can be so triggering to even the coolest, calmest, and most collected of us; the people we've known the longest are the ones who have seen all of our worst mistakes, biggest failures, and embarrassing missteps. They're the ones we're likely to have the most unresolved business with. While we can simply walk away from relationships with people who have disappointed us, it's a lot harder to walk away from family, even when they're the ones who remind us most of all the worst parts of ourselves that we wish we could forget.

It's a lot like the phrase "secrets make you sick." Only it's more like "awkward, uncomfortable family memories make you moody."

Conflict and communication are part of life. How you approach the conflict, rise to it, and solve it is what creates character. People (even your family) respect honesty and directness. In the words of Marianne Moore, "When one is frank, one's very presence is a compliment."

I haven't spoken to my family about "the Spain trip" (although now I'm sure I will); however, I have started communicating with them about other things—awkward, uncomfortable, tense things. Things like not wanting to work in the family business. Things like not liking the comments my mom makes about my relationship and friendships and hair color.

Because if Spain has taught me anything, it's that conflicts only get worse when you don't confront them head-on. It's better to have an honest, open conversation at the time than to spend the next eight years of your life tiptoeing around the subjects of dentistry, Spain, and tequila because you know that the mention of any of them will cause your stomach to drop to your knees.

That's not saying I'm always comfortable having these conversations. In fact, I usually dread them. But I've found a few tactics that alleviate the anxiety and help me decide if the conversation is, in fact, worth having. Conversations, like tequila shots, have a right place, right time, and a level where everything goes well and a point past which everything can go horribly wrong. So before I begin a conversation, I ask myself the following questions:

- What's the best thing that's likely to happen if I act?
- What's the worst thing that's likely to happen if I act?
- What's the best thing that's likely to happen if I do not act?
- What's the worst thing that's likely to happen if I do not act?

When I do have difficult conversations with anyone, not just my family, I'm also more aware of the type of language I'm using to deliver my message. I know how sensitive I am, and I also know that if you're going to have a conversation with someone about a messy topic, you want to avoid unnecessary injuries along the way.

The following tips don't just help you navigate uncomfortable conversations with your family members, but give you leverage when communicating with anyone you are looking to win over (for example, your boss, the hostess at Fig & Olive, clients, landlords):

- Avoid self-discounting language—When you start your conversation with words like "maybe I'm wrong" or "I might just be sensitive," you're discounting your statement and already either putting the other person on guard or giving them leverage to agree with you that yes, you are too sensitive. If you're going to start telling people how you really feel, don't water it down.

- Use "I" instead of "You" statements—When describing behavior that bothers you, reframe the way you say it. Phrases like "You're always late" put people on the offensive. When you say, "I feel hurt when I have to wait a long time" you state your case without offending or discrediting the other party. Because the conversation isn't about what they're doing wrong, it's about why what they're doing is upsetting you.

- Say "Thank you" instead of "Sorry"—This was a huge game-changer for me. When you're constantly apologizing, you're focusing on yourself, not the person you've hurt. "Sorry I'm late" just sounds like another haphazard excuse, a quick fix that relieves you of your guilt. "Thank you for waiting" changes the dynamic from excuser to appreciator. You are recognizing that they've done something for you and you're thanking them for it. People like to be appreciated and noticed. You'll be surprised how a quick thank-you changes their mindset.

If you can learn how to communicate what you really want to say in a way that reaches people on a level that makes them feel understood and appreciated, you'll see change in all your relationships. Because the moody woman is always lovable, even when she's done something unlikable.

UNDERSTAND YOU DON'T UNDERSTAND

Look into people's lives. Look into anyone's life.
There is always a nightmare somewhere.
—May Sarton, *The Bridge of Years*

In 1963, Elizabeth Taylor had just ended her fourth marriage and was starring in *Cleopatra* with the currently married Richard Burton. Within a year, the two were married at the Ritz in Montreal and their fame from *Cleopatra*, coupled with the drama of their private lives, made them the most famous couple in the world.

Like Kim and Kanye, they lived through extravagance. During the 1960s, they earned a combined $88 million and spent more than $65 million. They bought a fleet of Rolls-Royces, floors of luxury hotels, a private jet, a helicopter, and a multimillion-dollar yacht. And in 1969, every woman in America swooned a little when Richard Burton bought his wife the sixty-nine-carat Taylor-Burton Diamond for $1.1 million (adjusted for inflation, that's today's equivalent of $7 million).

Not only was it the world's most expensive diamond, it was the world's most sought-after diamond. When it was initially sold at auction, Burton lost in a bidding war with Cartier (Aristotle Onassis also lost). Accepting that he would have to go over his initial ground of $1 million, he made a deal with Cartier to buy it off them for $50,000 more than they'd spent on it.

Cartier, being a business above all else, agreed. They'd make $50,000 (the equivalent of $342,000 in today's dollars) profit in one day and stipulated, in a savvy marketing move, that the ring would first have to be displayed at Cartier boutiques in New York and Chicago before being handed off to its new owner. During that brief stint in Cartier's window, an estimated six thousand people stood in line to get a glimpse not just of the diamond, but of a symbol of the great passion they'd never have.

What does a million-dollar diamond look like? To many women, it looked like love. It looked like everything they dreamed about—that Hollywood love story. But no one in line, staring into the sparkling display, actually knew the true story of why Burton bought Taylor the most expensive diamond in the world.

Just a few weeks beforehand, the couple had been on vacation in Italy, sitting in a café, when Burton got into one of his angry drunken moods. When Elizabeth tried to cheer him up, asking him to hold her hand, he slapped it away, saying he wished she didn't have such large, ugly, masculine hands.

"Well, I guess you'll have to buy me a diamond so big it makes my large hands look small," she replied.

Burton would later write in his diaries, "That insult last night is going to cost me."

And the six thousand people lining up to see Elizabeth Taylor's million-dollar ring would never know that it wasn't a sign of devotion and love, but a gift of penance. That this ring was only the sign of their demise, a sparkling reflection of the drugs and the booze that would lead Elizabeth to eventually sell the diamond for $3 million (today's equivalent of $9 million) to finance her sixth husband's political campaign.

Why do I tell you this anecdote about Elizabeth Taylor? Because I want you to think of it next time you find yourself interpreting someone's actions. I want you to think of it when you think you know exactly why something happened and why someone did something. I want you to use it to remind yourself that most situations we perceive one way turn out to have a completely different story.

We make up stories all the time. Our friends didn't text us back because they don't like us. Our mom said that thing about our bathing suit because she thinks we're slutty. Our sister forgot our new boyfriend's name because she doesn't like him.

But take a beat and look at the other side. Maybe your friend didn't text back because she was overwhelmed. Maybe your mom said something about your bathing suit because she feels uncomfortable in her own. Maybe your sister forgot the name of your new boyfriend because she's been going through her own relationship issues and she's too distracted to remember.

Most of our moods stem from our own thoughts, which stem from our misconceptions and misinterpretations about what someone said or did. Perception is *everything*. How you perceive a situation, a dialogue, a moment, is the difference between getting into a mood and avoiding one.

According to Dr. Brian Boxer Wachler, your "perceptual intelligence" (PI) determines how you distinguish between reality and illusion. We never perceive the world directly. We let our memories and our emotions distort our perception of events and that's where our miscommunications and misunderstandings stem from.

Like the high-maintenance girl who thinks she's easygoing, I thought I had very high perceptual intelligence. I could sense when people were mad, upset, or uncomfortable, and I was quick to adjust my actions to make them happy. What I didn't realize, however, were two vital things: It wasn't my job to make everyone happy, and not everyone was always as uncomfortable or upset as I thought they were. As often as I was right, I was just projecting onto them and then creating my own discomfort.

I'm a dreamer. Jay says I have an active imagination. I use that imagination against myself more than I'd like—like always imagining the worst scenario possible. For example, a coworker and I attended the same meeting, yet I left depressed and she was on cloud nine.

"What's wrong with you?" she'd ask me.

"Didn't you hear what they said about the mockups? They hated them."

"They didn't say that at all! They said they were excited to see the other options."

"Yeah, hence, they hated them."

"No. It means they're happy with our work and want to see more."

It was clear my coworker had a positive outlook and I had a negative one. She spent the week in a good mood, working diligently and designing new options. I spent it stressed, snappy, and worried. In the end, it didn't matter what the clients meant. What shaped our experience was how we moved forward, how we took the information and used it to give the clients what they want: My coworker heard feedback, whereas I had heard criticism.

I needed something to help change my negative mindset— to stop perceiving everything as hostile or bad news, and to stop assuming that everything was a veiled or overt critique.

Maria Konnikova, author of *Mastermind: How to Think Like Sherlock Holmes*, describes ways to look at situations more objectively. "A helpful exercise is to describe the situation from the beginning, either out loud or in writing, as if to a stranger who isn't aware of any of the specifics—much like Holmes talks his theories through out loud to Watson. When Holmes states his observations in this way, gaps and inconsistencies that weren't apparent before come to the surface."

There's another way to do this as well. Skimming through my therapist's anxiety workbooks on his waiting room table, I found a chart. I took a photo of it on my phone, made some minor adjustments, and called it my "perception prep."

Anytime I face a situation, I draw up this chart and fill it out. It consists of four columns. The first is where you state the situation that's upsetting you. A recent one of mine would be: "My mom and I got into a fight." In the second column, write down your automatic thought about the situation: "I'm a terrible daughter. My mom hates me." In the third column, write evidence supporting the thought: "She yelled. I hung up the phone. She sounded angry." Now, write down the evidence against in the last column: "It's natural to fight. We've fought before and made up."

The Situation	Thoughts About The Situation	Evidence For	Evidence Against

The chart doesn't solve the situation, but it can help you better understand it. I eventually called my mom and apologized for this specific instance. And once I did that, it alleviated the amount of time I spent stewing over it. It saved me the hours I'd normally waste upset, rehashing the argument to my husband or friends, wondering if there was some loophole that exempted me from being a bad daughter, a bad wife, a bad friend.

The chart puts things in perspective. Okay, we had a fight. Now what? I call and apologize, and things go back to normal. This isn't any more of a big deal than our last fight. The apology and the admission of my mistake, however, took time to learn how to do.

LEARN TO APOLOGIZE

And apologies, once postponed, become harder
and harder to make, and finally impossible.
—Margaret Mitchell, *Gone with the Wind*

Now, I'm not telling you this story to ruin Princess Diana for you. I'm really not. But when it comes to mistakes, she wasn't without her own track record. And even though she'll always be the people's princess, that does not mean she was always a perfect wife, sister, and daughter-in-law.

I know this because in 1999, American investigative writer Sally Bedell Smith interviewed 150 people who knew Princess

Diana well and published one of the few unbiased biographies of her.

In *Diana in Search of Herself: Portrait of a Troubled Princess*, Smith brings up something a lot of us don't know about Princess Diana: She loved Prince Charles. She *wanted* to be married to him. In fact, she was so attracted to him, it didn't bother her that he was dating her older sister, Sarah, when she and Charles first met in 1977. And when it became clear that Sarah and Charles weren't compatible, it was the young, spirited sixteen-year-old Diana who had made up her mind that one day she would marry Prince Charles.

Three years later Charles and Diana met again and started dating. After meeting in person just thirteen more times, Charles proposed. Within six months they were married. But then cracks started to show. Diana, twelve years younger than Charles and new to the rules and regulations of Buckingham Palace, began acting out. She was insecure, jealous, and believed that Charles did not love her as he should. It didn't help that the British tabloids continually published stories of speculation about Charles's devotion to Camilla Parker Bowles.

Over time, Diana became more difficult and despondent. She wanted Charles's undivided attention and saw his preoccupation with his duties as rejection. Diana's good friend, interior designer Nicholas Haslam, recalls how her thoughts would lead her to spiral. "Diana would dwell on her perceived inadequacies, ponder the betrayals of her past and present, and think obsessively about her enemies, both real and imagined. Her thoughts would plunge her into tears and sometimes vengeful schemes. At such moments, she made her worst decisions."

One of these terrible decisions was when she decided to have secret tape-recorded sessions with a journalist looking to publish a confessional book about her private life. After years of feeling slighted, neglected, and unfairly portrayed in the tabloids and newspapers, Diana thought publishing a book about the "truth" behind her marriage and the royal family would show her side of things and cast her in a good light with the public. According to Smith, "Presented as the 'true story,' the book was actually her emotional perception of events, shaped by psychotherapy as well as astrological readings and alternative therapists who reinforced her efforts to assign blame." Her main fixation was on exposing Camilla as her husband's lover and having the public see her side of the story, and the marriage. *Diana: Her True Story* by Andrew Morton was published in June 1992.

Considering the fact that I'm nervous a story about getting drunk in Spain will damage my delicate relationship with my own mother, we can all surmise the damage a tell-all book about the queen and her son, published by the future queen, would do at Buckingham Palace. So when this book was published, no one could believe it. In a way, Princess Diana couldn't believe it either. She started lying to herself. Then lying to anyone who asked.

You know the type of lie. When you're so in shock you did something so stupid that you can't believe it could have been you. Naturally, the royal family, especially Charles, wanted to believe the same. So they asked Diana to sign a statement that condemned the book as fabricated and inaccurate. But she couldn't sign it. Not legally.

According to friends, Diana cried for weeks. When Charles tried to talk to her about it after reading the first excerpt in one of the newspapers, she fled in tears, escaping to London for the evening. She stopped talking to anyone who she previously asked to help with the book. She went into isolation. She was spiraling because there was no one to blame but herself. "I've done a really stupid thing. I have allowed a book to be written. I felt it was a good idea, a way of clearing the air, but now I think it was a very stupid thing that will cause all kinds of terrible trouble," Princess Diana lamented to her friend David Puttnam over dinner at a charity event.

Yet nowhere in Smith's account is there any mention of an apology. When Prince Philip wrote a series of letters to his daughter-in-law, both reprimanding and hoping to appeal to her by stating he understood marriage was difficult and Charles had his faults, Diana reacted defensively, hiring a lawyer to draft her replies. And six months after the book was published, Prime Minister John Major publicly announced Charles and Diana's "amicable separation" in a statement from the royal family.

If Diana had been able to take responsibility for the book, to apologize for the things she said and did, to own up to the actions caused by her moods, she may have been able to repair the damage, and her marriage, and most definitely would not have gone on to repeat the mistake again in a BBC *Panorama* interview four years later, which resulted in more scandal and the queen's request for her son's divorce.

Apologies are hard. When we feel hurt, misunderstood, or guilty, we tend to back away rather than confront our mistakes or our feelings. It's our ability to own up to our mistakes, however, that determines whether our relationships fail or succeed.

In 1986 professors John Gottman and Robert Levenson conducted laboratory experiments in an apartment on the University of Washington campus. They invited hundreds of married couples and asked them to solve a conflict in fifteen minutes. These interactions gave the researchers insight into which couples would stay together and which would divorce. Nine years later, they checked in on the couples and found their predictions—who would divorce and who'd stay together—to have been 90 percent accurate.

According to Gottman, it's inevitable that couples will fight. It's *how* we fight that determines how strong our marriage is. Anger isn't the cause of damaged relationships. It's the way we express our anger that leads to damage. "Anger only has negative effects in marriage if it is expressed along with criticism or contempt, or if it is defensive," Gottman says.

Among the couples who split, the vast majority took far longer to address a recent argument than those who stayed together, often leaving each other to stew in individual thoughts for hours or days after a fight. Conversely, couples who stayed together would typically discuss their arguments almost immediately after they'd happened.

According to Gottman, "Once you understand this, you will be ready to accept one of the most surprising truths about marriage: *Most marital arguments cannot be resolved.* Couples spend year after year trying to change each other's mind—but it can't be done. This is because most of their disagreements are rooted in fundamental differences of lifestyle, personality, or values." In fact, Gottman discovered that 69 percent of relationship problems are "perpetual" problems.

Whether a couple stayed together or divorced was based on multiple factors.

One of the six differences between couples who divorced and those who stayed together was the ability to "repair." Gottman defines "repairs" as "any statement or action—silly or otherwise—

that prevents negativity from escalating out of control." Couples who ended up staying together knew how to repair early and often. Couples who divorced were those who didn't know how to repair correctly or didn't try to repair at all. In fact, repairing is so important, the couples could survive four of the other "divorce traps," but if they couldn't repair, all was lost.

Marriage, like family, is rooted in your ability to communicate. Satir based her foundation of family models on the ability of the spouses to communicate. It's all connected and it's all necessary. If you can learn to apologize to your spouse, to communicate correctly, then you can apply that skill to the other relationships in your life—the relationships you can't control as easily.

Unlike in a friendship or marriage, you do not get to choose your biological family. You are born into a raffle, randomly selected and brought into a home with people who share the same gene pool as you but may share little else.

That is why families are the ultimate test in decorum. We've spent a lifetime trying to communicate, live, and control ourselves around people who bring out our biggest insecurities, worst memories, and bad moods. We've grown up battling people who seem to represent everything we stand against, people we're told we need to love but throughout most of our adolescence can't stand.

At a certain point, however, we have to learn to graduate from this dynamic if we want to have a positive, constructive relationship with family members. We must stop letting the pain of the past and the anxiety of the present determine how we behave around these people. Family will always be there. You can let them hang in the background, triggering you every holiday season, or you can harness the emotional intensity of this relationship, twist it into new forms, and not only show them the cool, lovable woman everyone else knows you to be, but also get to know them at their best. When you can learn to be in control of your reactions, understand what roles you are trapped in, and communicate on a level that's honest and vulnerable, you'll be able to bring out their hidden sides too—the sides they also so badly want to show to you.

THE MOOD TRANSFORMED

The name you choose for yourself is more your
own than the name you're born with.
—Candy Darling

I am what I am and I have to accept myself;
I was born like this, in this city, with this
dialect, without money; I will give what I can
give, I will take what I can take, I will endure
what has to be endured.
—Elena Ferrante, *The Story of a New Name*

Understanding is the beginning of healing.
—Sandra Cisneros, *Woman Hollering Creek*

THE MOOD:

THE BODY

Symptoms include: heaviness, numbness, inner chaos, and extreme desire for wine.

THE MOOD DESCRIBED

There were so many things that could be done to it or go wrong with it, this adult female body, that I was left feeling I would be better off without it.

—Margaret Atwood, *The Testaments*

How long will it feel like burning...

—Anne Carson, "Lines"

Didn't they know being a woman meant being at war?

—Catherine Lacey, *The Answers*

It was a bad night in a string of bad months. On top of not being able to sleep, I'd lost my appetite. I was down to one hundred pounds and the stress of my disappearing form on top of the stress of not being hungry made me less hungry. Lying in bed at two a.m., trapped in a vicious circle of thoughts, I tossed and turned. The mistakes, the memories, the missed moments replayed in my mind like a bad movie. Though I'd been praying for light to slip through the curtains, I didn't get out of bed until eight thirty. I blamed it on the Xanax, which I took out of desperation at three a.m. When I finally mustered the strength to get out of bed I walked to the bathroom, reflexively crossing my right hand over my chest toward the light switch as I moved in front of the mirror to evaluate my presence. Today was ugly. No use even trying. I used the toilet, dragged myself into the kitchen, and poured myself coffee. The sky was gray, and I was happy for it. At least the weather was right.

There was something stirring at the bottom of my soul. I felt it the way fishermen feel something on the line. I walked outside, crossed Metropolitan Avenue, and headed on my normal route to the subway. A truck passed. Then another. The revving engines like the throttled screams of a child. Covering my ears while everyone unaffectedly walked next to it hurled me further into my own tension. Was this what Jean Rhys felt when she wrote, "I must be very careful, today I have left my armor at home"?

I was relieved Sherry wasn't sitting behind the large block of white marble when I opened the glass door to the office. I wasn't as close to the receptionist as my coworkers Sam or Kendra, and the idea of making small talk was too much for me today. I was always flustered coming off the subway, wearing my long sleeves and jeans in the middle of July because I was tired of hearing how skinny I was. Everything felt bigger and harsher and more obtrusive. I felt weak and fragile, simultaneously hoping no one noticed while also wishing someone would ask me *what's wrong* so I could melt into the floor, the words sliding out like mud: *everything*.

I wasn't surprised when Kendra asked me why I looked different after sitting across from me in the staff meeting. I knew it was because my face was stretched like it always was when I felt this way. It's the look I have when I'm fighting something within myself. A gaunt, wide-eyed look. I looked older. I felt older. I felt completely aged. But inside this was newborn rage and agitation, with the energy of a child, asking for a fight.

When Sam decided to take the L train back to Brooklyn with me, I learned this child was just looking for a cry. A big, loud wail. As we stood there, our hands grasping the pole that ran from the floor to the ceiling, Sam asked, "Have you decided if you're going on a honeymoon?"

"Maybe, I don't know, we've just been so busy ever since the wedding," I murmured with a flat tone.

"What about kids, do you plan on having any?" he then asked.

Whether this conversation was devised to get to the crux of the dig or it was Sam's twenty-two-year-old naivety, I'll never know. All I do know is that when I said, "Eventually," he responded, "Interesting," while gazing at the subway ads, leaving a pause in the conversation before continuing. "Because Sherry says she thinks you look too skinny and there might be a problem *there*," motioning to the thin rail that was my body.

"Sherry can go to hell!" I said. Except I never did get "hell" out the way I intended because the tears were flowing and the commuters were looking and Sam had this expression on his face that told my reasonable, rational self that his comment had not been meant in "that way." But it was too late, the thing at the bottom of my soul was now coming up.

The man sitting below me, the pages of his book liable to drench, sweetly demanded I switch with him. As I sat, Sam continued to apologize. "I didn't mean it like that," he kept trying to reassure me. Only I thought he really did. I had been attacked, out of nowhere. This felt more painful than it should have, like a papercut that's barely visible. We rode silently, or I cried and sat and he stood and looked out of the black window behind me, until the train arrived at Bedford and I walked off. I cried the seven blocks back to my apartment. Hot, delicious tears. I was crying but I was happy because it was over.

Except it wasn't. The next day I woke to the same feeling. There was momentary relief upon realizing it was Saturday and I wouldn't have to face Sam, but after that passed, the knot was still there, clamped against my soul. The sky was still gray. The feeling still sat there, with no reason or explanation. Until the next time I used the bathroom, only to see that all-too-familiar red line.

WHAT THE MOOD IS TELLING YOU

But wait, didn't I just have my period? Maybe because I didn't keep a calendar, or because it still seemed unreal that my body bled out once a month, I'd always had trouble keeping track of my cycles. But I had never been this off before. When I finally did start keeping track, I realized why I was so taken aback each time. I was getting my period twice a month.

Two months later I sat in the waiting room of the Polish gynecologist in Greenpoint—the one with orange carpet and fluorescent lights, in the green building with the awning next to the Polish bakery. Three men in lab coats were casually walking in and out of doors, and when a tall, young, blond one with a square jaw walked out, I prayed. Those prayers were answered when the eighty-five-year-old with no semblance of a jaw called my name. I couldn't handle a handsome gynecologist right now.

At his desk he put a white strip in the cup of urine I handed him. I told him about my two periods, and he asked me how long it had been happening for, and confessed I thought a few months, and then three minutes apparently went by because he took the white strip out, placed it on a white paper towel, and confirmed I wasn't pregnant. (Well yeah, I'm getting two periods.) After moving me to the exam table and closing a yellow-and-red-checkered curtain around it, he confirmed that this physiological event was nothing serious. I just had insufficient progesterone, which meant I wasn't producing enough of that specific hormone, so my body was confused and was producing two eggs—skipping stages. He told me it was most likely a result of stress and with medication I could rectify it. It was common.

It didn't feel common. It felt like the last blow. More medication? More regulation? More periods?? It felt like I couldn't even get my body to function correctly. My life was out of sorts, and now my body was following. Or maybe my life was out of sorts because of my body?

It's all related, isn't it? Stress of the mind is manifested in the body. It's a cyclical, symbiotic relationship. I wasn't sleeping because I was stressed, which was causing me to get my period twice, which was making me extra hormonal, which would create more tension and stress, which would lead to me not sleeping well. I saw the cycle repeating until I died. It was all related. The body. The mind. The moods. I couldn't fix one of them without understanding all of them.

Candace Pert was an American neuroscientist and pharmacologist known for her work on the unity of the body and mind. One of her most famous discoveries was the opiate receptor, the cellular binding site for endorphins in the brain. According to Pert, emotions are not solely the product of your brain, but are expressed, experienced, and stored in what she called your "bodymind." All of our painful memories—failure, disappointments, suffering, loss—are hidden away or suppressed in our bodyminds, to be retrieved, reformed, and released, or ignored and left to fester, promoting physical ailments and unexplained changes in the body.

In Pert's book *Molecules of Emotion: The Science Behind Mind-Body Medicine* she advocated a holistic approach to medicine, arguing that our physical and emotional health are tied. What happens in our minds shows up in our bodies. According to Pert, "Virtually all illness, if not psychosomatic in foundation, has a definite psychosomatic component."

My body, I realized, needed as much attention as my mind. For years, I'd ignored my body, not understanding that it was an extension of the thoughts and feelings I was trying so hard to grasp.

There are certain times when the mood is not about a person or an expectation or an event. It's not the past or the future. It's just me. And it took me the longest to figure this mood out, when it should have been the most obvious one. But it wasn't obvious, because I was ignoring it. I was ashamed to admit how little I knew about myself. How little control I had over my body. How I couldn't get it to sleep right, eat right, bleed right.

It was time to grow up. Time to take a look under the hood of the car. "The body," said Martha Graham, "is a sacred garment. It's your first and your last garment; it is what you enter life in and what you depart life with, and it should be treated with honor." Honor was something I either lost or never had, and now I was going to get it.

ACKNOWLEDGE YOUR CYCLES

Dogs are wise. They crawl away into a quiet corner and lick their wounds and do not rejoin the world until they are whole once more.

—Agatha Christie, *The Moving Finger*

In order to stop having the two periods, I had to pay attention to my body. The doctor was vague, like all doctors are, assuming I knew as much about female anatomy as he did. I live in my body, I should understand it better than anyone. Only I didn't. I was approaching thirty and didn't understand it at all.

When I found out what happens to the female body throughout the course of a single month, I thought of Brenna Twohy's quote: "What do you call womanhood if not endurance? The ways we withstand that which we did not believe withstandable..." My moods and emotions were at the mercy of a body that was carrying out complex processes, and I wasn't enduring it, I was actively resisting it.

I think we all do that a bit. We've all reflexively denied our femaleness for fear all our thoughts, emotions, and feelings will be reduced to the label of *hormonal woman*. We refuse to admit we feel differently when we have our periods, because history has taught us that we won't be taken seriously. So we reject it. We vehemently deny it. And it's true that people will try to use it against us, but the people who do are the ones who don't understand it. If we understood ourselves, and were honest with ourselves, we'd know that the female body is a highly complex and incredible organism and, as a result, we will experience some side effects. It's our divine right.

Unlike a man's, the female body goes through a cycle of hormone changes every month. Because of this ever-changing cycle, women are underrepresented in medical trials. The length of time it will take a new drug to metabolize in the body is complicated to predict for women because our bodies are always in different stages. So why is it so bad to admit that some stages are harder than others? For almost six months I'd been getting my period twice, which until recently I didn't understand meant I was experiencing PMS twice a month.

Accepting PMS was like accepting that the pain in my teeth was a cavity or the throb in my side was appendicitis; it was a condition of the body that was as real as any other pain. Female hormones fluctuate so massively over the course of our menstrual cycle, we have anywhere from two to four different physiologies. Except during pregnancy, there is no other time when a human's body goes through such drastic changes. Our skin, which is filled with estrogen receptors, undergoes a wave of fluctuations in estrogen and progesterone levels the week before menstruation. The result is excess deposits of lipids and oil that sit on the surface, giving us a gray, greasy look that's perfect for creating blemishes. We feel like a different person because we are a different person, inside and out.

The week before menstruation, the female body's total daily energy expenditure rises and insulin resistance increases along with our appetite and cravings for sweets. This week before menstruation is known as the luteal phase of ovulation, during which 75 percent of women report experiencing PMS.

During this time, we tend to have higher negative affect and higher physiological reactivity than at any other stage of a period. Research has also shown that when it comes to cognition tests, women in this phase demonstrated lower performance in tasks that required focused attention and higher vigilance. They also made more errors; however, the errors could be because the women were answering faster and with less regard, suggesting a degree of impulsivity.

The desire to jump out of my skin, the heightened emotional state, the restlessness—it was all part of being a menstruating woman. And in pretending it wasn't happening I was denying myself the sanity the facts brought. An awareness that I was supposed to feel this way. That it was an inevitable side effect of *my time of the month*.

Is it so bad to admit that sometimes our moods and feelings simply stem from these fluctuations? Are we that determined not to let anybody, even ourselves, know that we feel different? That there's a few days out of the month when maybe the irritability you have is nothing more than a change in your chemical structure? Instead of always trying to fight it, why aren't we leaning into it?

Leaning into it meant respecting it. I was too old to be surprised by my period every month. Too smart to be this naïve about it. In order to get it back on track, the doctor had specific instructions. I had to start taking the medicine on the last day of my next period. My next *real* period. Not the second one I might get two weeks from now. To do that, I had to pay attention. And it was this tracking, this buying of a calendar and taking note, that began a new chapter for me and my body. Losing my natural cycle was like an awakening. I would not mess up again. I would take it seriously, this business of being a woman.

Downloading an app made it easy, and seeing my cycles, the way they worked and came like clockwork, gave me a newfound sense of my female power. The way it worked when I wasn't looking. The way it could stop working if I was not respecting it. The way it would do what it needed to do only when I gave it what it needed. I felt a sense of pride when my period came on the day it should. I could ride the wave, not smash up against it. There was rhythm and routine. And routine is what I was missing from my life.

The routine brought an understanding of what was happening and why. I stopped fearing the feelings that previously made no sense. When I felt the pangs of discomfort or the swings of emotion, I could look in my calendar and assure myself that this was how it was supposed to be. These were just natural symptoms of an inevitable process. And when I understood the routine of my own body, I could start building comforts around it.

It was Rosario who taught me this. In the six months I lived in her two-bedroom apartment during my semester abroad in Madrid, I learned little about her life. Because she spoke no English and I understood one out of every four Spanish words, our conversations were more high-level exchanges. I understood she was forty-five, not married but had met the love of her life; it didn't work out because he was an apple and she was an orange. I knew she was studying to be a lawyer after quitting her job at the family business, and that she had eight months until the law exam, the results of which would determine if her years of studying and taking exchange students to support herself had paid off, or if she would have to return back to the family business with her tail between her legs.

I knew that Rosario was a private person. But more than private, she was disciplined. The way she lived was precise. She was never late. Never early. Through the thin wall between our bedrooms, I heard her alarm go off at six o'clock every morning. Only one beep. Never two. Never snoozed.

Breakfast was always laid out before I got to the kitchen. The same thing every morning: loaf of bread, boiled eggs, and jams. By the time I dragged myself into the kitchen she was already in her makeshift office in the corner of the living room, studying. She had an inner drive that superseded everything else—

socializing, drinking, procrastinating. Her dedication made me ashamed whenever I'd try to sneak out in my red bodycon ASOS dress to head to Kapital or some seedy bar in La Latina. She'd always look up from her book with a motherly expression and ask where I was going, then tell me I was going to be cold in such a short dress. When I'd return the next morning she'd be at her desk, exactly where I'd left her.

And then one day she wasn't. I'd arrived home from school for my midafternoon snack and siesta and she was on the couch, the sound of Spanish soaps echoing from the TV that was never on, a cup of hot tea in her lap and a half-empty box of biscuits out. "*La regla*," she told me, and I nodded like I understood before going into my room to look up yet another word I didn't know.

I found it interesting that the word for "period" in Spanish was the same as the word for "rule." Because that's how Rosario was following it. The rule of her body. Over the course of six months I saw it happen six times. Same Spanish soaps. Same tea. Same biscuits. And she'd always say the same thing when I saw her. "*La regla*"—as if it were some designated holiday.

She owned it without any shame. This was her time of the month. Her dedication, her drive, was no match for the physical needs of her womanhood. In fact, her period was a designated stopping point for her, the break she'd learned to make herself take. Her experience reminded me of a Native American tribe I read about known as the Yurok whose aristocratic women celebrated their periods together, with rituals. They saw it as a time to purify themselves. I wondered if all Spanish women were taught to celebrate their periods the same way the Yurok women did. Or maybe it was just something women learned as they got older. Maybe it took time to learn to honor your body.

It wasn't until I understood and accepted what my body could do that I came to respect what it couldn't. Only when I accepted that my body is this incredibly complex biological miracle did I also accept that this makes me delicate. The price of being female is paid in blood, and before battle, we must nourish ourselves.

I can't take off from work for five days, can't stop my duties, but I can give myself a break. I can soothe myself when I feel sad or angry or worked up with the reminder that these feelings are another test of womanhood that I will pass. I remember that it's okay to go straight home and lick my wounds. To be a little distant and edgy and uncomfortable. The rule of my body dictates that I take care of myself and return to the world when I am whole again.

FIND YOUR TRUE BEDTIME

A good day for me is a night. I don't enjoy the daylight hours. I'm not a morning person...or an afternoon person.

—Fran Lebowitz

I felt the same way about sleep as I did about my period. I couldn't do something that was natural and normal and easy for everyone else. This shame manifested as a restless agitation the moment I felt the gold light cascading through the windows. I hated the idea of the world leaving without me. I dreaded lying in that dark room. Every night was twenty hours long.

I've never been good at falling asleep. Since high school I'd been in the habit of taking my laptop to bed like a blanket. Since moving to New York I felt the disease progressing, the laptop no longer adequate. Now I needed drugs.

Jay falls asleep naturally and without struggle. That wasn't in my nature. My body opposed it, pulsing alive the moment I hit the mattress. I read somewhere that men fall asleep faster than women because they carry less throughout the day. That fact ran through my mind whenever I'd look over at Jay's sleeping body. I felt betrayed and insulted at how easy it was for him to turn off. How quickly he unpacked.

It makes sense to me that adults are always asking each other how they slept. How someone slept can be at the crux of how they feel. If they slept well, whatever is wrong is about something else. If they slept poorly, whatever is wrong is because of that. Most of the women I knew had the same relationship to sleep as I did. I saw it in my mother. If I passed my parents' bedroom in the night, she was always the one sitting up, the glow of the TV on her face. She was the alert one when we'd sneak in at two a.m. And she was the one usually lamenting how she hadn't slept. I always thought it was because women were tied to the moon. And while I still believe the moon is female and connected to us the same way it's connected to the tides, I also know there's a scientific explanation: Our brains are hardwired to take longer to fall asleep.

According to professor Jim Horne, an expert in sleep science, women's propensity to multitask—take care of the kids; work; keep track of the house, bills, relationships, friendships—overworks the brain and requires more downtime. This multitasking behavior creates higher momentum, which means we need more of a runway to slow down. This is why women are more than twice as likely to have trouble falling asleep than men. There's also the increase of cortisol during our premenstrual phase, the same hormone we produce when we're stressed, keeping us even more alert through the night.

I understood that my sleep patterns were affecting me, but I didn't know how to fix them. I couldn't sleep because I was scared of all the problems I was creating by not being able to sleep.

Insomnia is built on this irony. According to late Harvard professor Daniel M. Wegner, insomnia is caused by the brain's inability to stop thinking about itself. And the more we worry about not being able to sleep, the more our brain won't let us. This phenomenon was tested on a group that was told they'd be judged on how fast they could relax. By thinking about needing to relax, the body constantly monitored itself and made relaxing impossible. When it comes to sleep, the problem gets worse each night you don't sleep well because you're stressing that much more about needing sleep.

Charles Morin, a professor of psychology at Université Laval in Québec, spent ten years studying behavioral modification techniques for insomnia. His research focused on cognitive behavioral therapy (CBT) as a treatment, as he believed restless nights stemmed from our fears of restlessness and the cure lay not in any external answer but, like most answers, within. Before using the CBT model, he asked patients to look into their sleep hygiene—things in their lifestyle and bed preparation routine that could be changed to improve sleep. Diet, exercise, temperature, and lighting were all factors the subjects had control over when it came to better sleep and Morin believed should be noted and regulated before diving into the real work. Imagine starting with a clean slate. There was no use trying to help people cure their insomnia if they weren't aware of the simple changes they could make that may be the underlying culprit of their restless nights. Of course, they were all the things I'd read about and tried already.

No caffeine after ten a.m. No alcohol. More exercise. No computer lights in bed. Like with every diet or attempt to clean up my life, I would try these changes for a few days, then revert to my old ways. No amount of blackout shades or white noise machines or meditation techniques was going to lull me into unconsciousness. My problem wasn't my environment, it was my brain. Even if the blue light from the screen was keeping me awake, I couldn't stop it because I was too scared to sleep without it. I couldn't attempt to fix my sleep hygiene until I fixed the bigger issue. My restlessness was born out of fear. Fear of my thoughts; fear of loneliness; fear of failing, once again, at something I should naturally know how to do.

Research has found that CBT therapy reduces false beliefs about sleep. These false beliefs include unrealistic expectations about sleep (I need eight hours every night), exaggerations of the consequences of missed sleep (I'm damaging my health and going to die because I'm not sleeping well), and faulty thinking about the cause of not being able to sleep (genetic factors, underlying health issues). These fears are what keep the mind awake and in this perpetual loop of insomnia. We can't get to sleep because we're scared of why we can't get to sleep. To tackle my issues with sleep, I had to tackle my fear. And only when I threw out the Xanax and the NyQuil and decided to face the dark was I able to understand what the fear was and how to overcome it.

ACCEPT DREAMS AS JOBS

One of the reasons I hated falling asleep was because I was scared of my dreams. I didn't like not having control over the movie that played in my mind. I didn't like that when I closed my eyes, there was a chance I could be hurled into an uncomfortable scenario. And most importantly, I hated that I would carry the weight and feeling of my dreams with me like an old gym bag for days on end.

There are multiple reasons people are prone to remember their dreams. Research shows that those who can remember their dreams share similar tendencies toward daydreaming, creative thinking, and introspection. Those who don't remember their dreams are more focused on external events—live less in the mind. There's also research highlighting that those with irregular sleep patterns are abruptly waking during REM sleep (the part of our sleep cycle in which we dream), causing them to recall more throughout the night. If I didn't remember my dreams it probably wouldn't have mattered, but I was one of those people who did. And that wasn't going to change.

What changed was that I learned our dreams aren't supposed to be nice. They aren't there to entertain us, to pull us into a whimsical world of our favorite things. Our dreams are there to do a job—to do the emotional processing for us, to clean up all the emotional baggage we didn't deal with throughout the day.

Within a day, we experience hundreds of encounters, awkward moments, clashes, feelings. We don't, however, sit down to process all of these. Our dreams process those emotional moments for us. According to sleep researcher Rosalind D. Cartwright, "In this way, dreaming diffuses the emotional charge of the event and so prepares the sleeper to wake ready to see things in a more positive light, to make a fresh start."

Our dreams aren't supposed to be magical. Our dreams are the midnight crew that comes in to clean up the mess. The stains and chipped paint and overflowing garbage—the tiny infractions and slights you incurred throughout the day. By trying to re-create memories, our dreams are trying to hash out unresolved emotional conflicts. The brain, however, can never replicate an exact memory, so it makes up a new one that has the same feeling.

You didn't slash your husband's tires, but something happened that had the equivalent effect—or that made you want to respond in that way. Maybe you said something that was hurtful, the words replaced with a knife in your dream because your brain didn't remember the words but rather the sharpness of them. Maybe another important male figure in your life hurt you during the day but left you unable to respond or retaliate. It's why we wake up in the morning with a weird feeling about someone and sometimes have a hard time letting it go.

Before understanding this, I felt my subconscious was betraying me. I was scared of it. Scared of all the monsters and feelings it wanted to bring out when I was caught off guard. Now I understand my dreams are just trying to help me. They're there to put all the emotions, memories, and feelings I don't want to deal with to bed.

> Yes, I had nightmares—children do. After all,
> it takes some time to get used to being alive.
> And how else, except in the clarity of dreams,
> are you supposed to see the world all around
> you that's hidden by the light of day?
> —Deborah Eisenberg, *All Around Atlantis*

STOP TRYING SO HARD

I used to blame Jay for my restless nights. We'd been to-gether five years when I told him my goal in life was a two-bedroom apartment so I could have my own space. I even suggested we live like Frida Kahlo and Diego Rivera, in two separate houses connected by a bridge. I'd read an article about how married couples with separate bedrooms got along better and stayed married longer. The sleep patterns of our partners—their tossing, turning, and snoring—can affect our sleep and we unconsciously build animosity toward them for it.

Besides his tossing and turning, I believed my inability to sleep was because Jay was forcing me to go to bed early. He was a morning person and I was a creature of the night. I needed to be able to stay up, with the lights on, doing my thing. He was opposing my natural rhythm.

Then Jay started traveling for work and that theory fell apart. I'd still get into bed around nine and put on Netflix and find myself wide awake at one a.m., having binged an entire season of *Grace and Frankie*. I had the room, the bed, the night to myself and I was still having trouble.

According to Morin, that's because I was getting in bed at nine and trying to will myself to sleep. Even though I knew I was a night owl, I turned off the lights and put on my shows expecting to fall asleep the same time Jay did. But it's impossible to make yourself sleep on command. In fact, when we try to force ourselves to sleep is when it backfires on us. Changing my habit of forcing myself to get ready for bed at nine p.m. also brought back some of the love I used to have for the night.

MAKE THE NIGHT SPECIAL

When Jay got back from traveling, I told him that it was nothing against him, but I was going to try sleeping on the couch. I'd make the couch into my bed so I could stay up without bothering him. This alleviated the pressure I didn't know I was carrying to bed every night—the guilt about keeping him awake with my restlessness. I'd worried every time he tossed and turned that it was because of me.

Sitting outside in the living room, I remembered why I was a night owl. I started lighting candles, playing my jazz, writing in my journals, and reading again. It was my private time. And the more I did it, the less nervous I felt as the sun went down. You have to get into bed, or get into your nighttime routine, thinking about how luxurious it is. This is your time. There's no stress. No pressure. Just you and the bed and whenever you're ready. You can curl up and watch your favorite show. I reestablished my relationship with the darkness—my connection to the moon. I stopped fearing the night and started getting excited for it.

ACCEPTANCE OF BEING A BAD SLEEPER

When I started getting excited about the night again, I began rejecting the overwhelming anxiety I had about what my late bedtime was doing to my health. I concluded that stressing about not sleeping was definitely worse, in the long run, than not getting a full eight hours every night. Charles Morin and researchers have concluded that the anxiety of loss of sleep is the main contributor to insomnia.

When you believe all your problems stem from lack of sleep, you can't sleep because of all the problems. But the "right" amount of sleep, like red meat and carbs and all the other things we hear are killing us, is relative. People survive on four to six hours a night for their entire lives. People who get ten hours of sleep can still feel tired during the day. Scientists believe that genetics play a role in how long we need to sleep per day and how predisposed we are to the effects of it. Some of us need more sleep than others, and while sleep affects our mood, it wasn't the catalyst to all my problems.

Like the Stoics, I accepted my destiny. I would rather die young from a life of late nights than live a long, miserable life in the dark. Whatever was going to kill me was going to kill me. Of all the vices to have, lack of sleep wasn't the worst one. And with that acceptance, I went into the living room with my books and my movies and my work, prepared to stay up until two, three, four a.m. . . . only to pass out before eleven.

GIVE YOUR BODY A ROUTINE

If you do the same thing every day at the same time for the same length of time, you'll save yourself from many a sink. Routine is a condition of survival.

—Flannery O'Connor

I want to say my drinking habit was perpetuated by my sleeping habit, and that when I started sleeping better, I started drinking less. I wanted to believe that would happen so much that I announced to Jay that I would be partaking in dry January. New Year's Eve would mark my last sip (binge) of alcohol. Now that I could sleep, I didn't need alcohol to knock me out.

Only it turned out that I needed it for other things. Long days, nerves, to have fun, to talk to people. Ten days in I was sneaking shots or chugging two glasses of wine before Jay could walk through the door. I thought that when I started sleeping better and felt less stressed, my appetite would come back. But it didn't. Then it would for a day. Then I'd get cramps two days later. Then I'd be bloated. Then I wouldn't be hungry. Was something wrong with me that was creating these symptoms and stress, or was my stress still affecting my body?

My friend Clare believed it was my body affecting my brain. She said it was happening to her. She'd gone to the doctor and asked them to do every blood test possible. She figured she must be anemic or allergic to gluten or wheat or pollen. Something was wrong and she wanted answers.

The blood tests came back normal. Her doctor, however, had a recommendation. *Try cutting out sugar*, she told Clare.

"And how are you feeling now?" I asked her.

"Well, it's only been a few weeks, but I definitely feel a difference in my mood. But maybe it's just psychosomatic."

"Yeah," I said, "but if our body and mind are connected, isn't everything psychosomatic?"

Psycho means "mind." *Soma* means "body." The term *psycho-somatic*, which we've been taught to associate with "imaginary" illnesses, refers to the physiological connection between the mind and the body—a connection that is becoming more concrete and indisputable by the day.

There is emerging evidence highlighting how our brain function is affected by the microbes within us. **Definite links have been found between an unbalanced gut microbiota and depression, anxiety, and mood disorders.** Microbiologist and neuroscientist Ruairi Robertson spent years researching connections between our stomachs and brains, specifically how our intestines and the microbes within them can influence our physical and mental health. Through his research he discovered that humans don't just have one brain, but two. When we're born, we are smothered in an invisible coating of microbes from our mother's birth canal. These bacteria grow to form a three-pound invisible organ inside the large intestine known as our microbiome. This is our second brain and it controls as much of our physical and mental functions as the brain in our heads, which, interestingly, also weighs three pounds.

Microbiome refers to all the different bacteria, viruses, and fungi that live within the body. Our health, immune system, and general functioning rely on the delicate balance of our diverse microbiome. According to Robertson, the types of bacteria inside you may control the way you think and feel.

The nineteenth-century Russian scientist Ilya Mechnikov claimed that our gut microbiota, or gut bacteria, were essential for human health, and the right balance of microbes inside us could help stave off disease. In the mid-1800s he studied a group of people in Eastern Europe living especially long lives. He noted that they all drank bacteria-fermented milk every day. He began drinking this bacterial-fermented milk and lived until the age of seventy-one—at a time when the life expectancy was forty.

Our microbiomes are the center point of our immune systems, meaning a disturbance in the gut can cause subtle immune reactions all around the body, which if prolonged can affect brain health. Neurotransmitters like serotonin are also produced in the gut. In fact, 90 percent of all serotonin is produced in the intestine. If your microbiome is off or your gut has a bad reaction to certain types of food, you'll feel it in your mood. Mechnikov argued that some lifestyles that weaken our gut bacteria, such as a diet low in fiber, can make us more vulnerable to chronic diseases and stress. A 2011 study titled "Linking Long-Term Dietary Patterns with Gut Microbial Enterotypes" found that noticeable shifts in microbial composition can be observed after as little as twenty-four hours. This shift was seen with people cutting out sugars and simple carbs and feeling more emotionally stable.

When I went to the doctor to ask for blood tests, he said no. Well, he said yes, but then he asked if I wanted to pay the hundreds of dollars to have every kind of blood test, like Clare had. He said the best way to figure out why I wasn't gaining weight, and whether there really was an issue with my body, was to start by keeping a log. This would give us a set of data points to work with; that way we could just test allergies to the types of food I was consuming, along with ruling out things like tapeworm or anemia. He also wanted to keep track of how many calories I was consuming. If it was a simple issue of my just not eating enough, we could figure out a diet plan that filled in the gaps.

To keep track for two weeks I had to pay much closer attention to what I was eating, and almost immediately started to notice some things. I was only eating when I started to feel faint or hangry, at such random times that I barely knew what I was eating and when. I had no consistency to my diet. I quickly realized the reason I was never hungry for dinner was because I was eating lunch at two p.m. My stomach was growling at ten p.m., not only keeping me awake but also causing me to reach for things like doughnuts and Cup Noodles. I was skipping breakfast or eating a banana in the morning and calling it healthy. Sitting in the waiting room before the follow-up appointment, I had the urge to leave the office for an "emergency," print off another blank log, and fill it in as a normal person would. I wouldn't be lying, just tidying it up a bit, making it a bit less obvious. But then what was the point? I was trying to figure out where I was going wrong, not cover more up. The log didn't lie. The log exposed me, and it wasn't some medical mystery.

"You're eating," the doctor said. "You're just not eating well. Just because you had a salad for lunch doesn't mean you had a good lunch. You're not getting enough calories in a salad to offset the calories you're burning off throughout the day." He suggested two tablespoons of flaxseed per day to give me an easy boost of two hundred calories. He suggested putting them in a smoothie for a quick breakfast. Then he suggested more fatty omega acid–rich foods like salmon and yogurt. I wrote his suggestions down on a notepad and left the office with a renewed sense of purpose.

You know when you splurge on an expensive new blouse or designer pants and it makes you want to throw out your closet and redo your whole wardrobe? That's how I felt with my new diet. I wanted to be in control. I wanted to start fresh and give myself only the best. I wanted to glow from the inside out.

I bought a blender and flaxseed and coconut water and Greek yogurt and started getting up earlier to make myself a smoothie with a side of vitamin D pills and fish oil. Before leaving for work I remembered to grab a protein bar for when I was ready for breakfast. (I've yet to meet a woman who jumps out of bed hungry at six a.m.) I started packing my lunch and planning out my weekly dinner recipes on Sunday, excited to go to the store. It felt good to take care of myself. It felt good to no longer be worried about what I was going to do for my next meal. My weight (or lack of it) was no longer this burden I was carrying around. I could let it go while also, finally, putting on the right kind.

While the log was designed to make me think about what and when I was eating, it had the opposite effect. It incorporated food, like my period and sleep, into a routine I no longer had to think about. Because it was part of my life in a strict and set way, I didn't feel like I was chasing it.

The chase is what this mood, this chapter, boils down to. Like an ouroboros, the mythological Greek serpent that eats its own tail, we are devouring ourselves. When we feel in flux, when there's no set schedule, no order, no care with the edges, we become chaotic. When we're chaotic, we lose things—keys, wallets, periods, sleep, weight. And in losing these things, we become more anxious and chaotic, making us lose more weight and more sleep, and the cycle continues.

While I'd always believed monotony was worse than death, routine, as Flannery O'Connor pointed out, is a condition of survival. Routine is what gives you back your footing.

Before I knew it, I'd built my life into a routine. I was getting up at the same time every morning, giving myself an hour I'd never had before to adjust and move and greet the day with a sharper mind. I was taking time to make breakfast and lunch, and in doing that, I was eating better. I was being strict with myself, allowing myself wine, but only starting on Wednesday. And that wine tasted better. (Also, because I was drinking less I could buy nicer bottles.) And when I started to feel the unexplainable moods or feelings, I would feel a sense of joy. Because I knew it was just my period coming. And I'd buy myself my favorite chocolate bar and look forward to bingeing on the shows I had waited to watch and scheduled for this time. Everything in my life had purpose now, felt special now, felt as it should be. And in creating order in my life, I created order in my body.

THE MOOD TRANSFORMED

To take things easy, not to fight against the ebb and flow of life, but to give way to it—that was what was needed. It was this tension that was all wrong.
> —Katherine Mansfield, "At the Bay"

Now I'm going to take care of *myself*.
> —Juliette Drouet

And there is nothing like a cheerful mind for keeping the body in health.
> —Anne Brontë, *Agnes Grey*

THE MOOD:

UNFORESEEN
CIRCUMSTANCES

Symptoms include: road rage, airport meltdowns,
and the desire to scream "life isn't fair."

THE MOOD DESCRIBED

I am tired of measure, control, doing the right thing. A part of me would like to tear something apart and howl like a wolf!

—May Sarton, *Recovering: A Journal*

I feel bad about my struggle, because it is nothing compared to other people's struggles and yet it still hurts.

—Melissa Broder, "I Don't Feel Bad
About My Neck"

There's something off about that girl. Border-line. Any little shock could push her right over the edge.

—Margaret Atwood,
"Gertrude Talks Back"

It was my twenty-eighth birthday. A few days earlier, when Jay had asked what I wanted to do, I think he half expected me to say "Nothing." At first I did say "Nothing." But fifteen minutes later I walked back into the bedroom, stood in the doorway, and told him that I wanted to get a cocktail. Specifically, a cocktail at the Plaza. I wanted to put on tights and a dress and red lipstick and take the subway to Fifth Avenue, past the corner of Central Park, through the smoke flying off the yellow hot dog stands, across the street with the horse buggies that make me sad, and onto the red carpeted steps of *the Plaza*.

Jay had first asked me on a Wednesday, and by Saturday morning I realized I didn't just want it, I *needed* it. It was a cold, gray day in February and I felt as dead as the landscape outside. It had been a long December and even longer January, and I'd spent both months in sweatpants, locked inside my increasingly cramped apartment. The five blocks I ventured to the grocery store and the pharmacy and to grab a drink at the bar felt less like my neighborhood and more like a prison yard. In. Out. In. Out. Gray concrete pavement below gray skies. I needed to get out of Brooklyn. Out of my routine. The rest of winter stretched before me like a vast wasteland and the Plaza was starting to feel more and more like a soft warm light that would revitalize me. If we couldn't go away to some tropical island to refresh ourselves, the Plaza, in my opinion, was the next best thing. A small fix to keep me going.

The same way people love Disney World, I love hotels. They feel magical and safe and like a piece of home. When I first moved to New York, when I had no boyfriend or friends or steady job and the loneliness filled my bones like lead, I'd find myself drifting into them without thinking. Half-mesmerized, I'd glide through the revolving doors into the cool marble hallways, drop my backpack on a plush velvet couch, and just rest. The load, the pain, the fear would be whisked away in the rush of happy families sailing by in their mittens and scarves. The smell of jasmine and crisp linen would wash through me, cleansing my spirit, and the soft light that poured from the ceiling onto a bouquet of flowers would welcome me home. I'd sit for hours, no one bothering me, no one asking if I needed a table, a drink, a room. For all they knew I was just another guest, and like every real guest, I was supposed to feel comfortable.

Of all the hotels in New York, the Plaza was my favorite. I loved the copper roof that oxidized into the mint-green color so characteristic to New York. I loved the way it sat on the corner of Central Park and Fifth Avenue, so grand, so stately, so poised. I loved how on the other side of the revolving door was frenzy, cabs honking and tour guides selling, but inside was quiet. I loved that no matter what was going on outside, none of it mattered inside. Everything was always the same. It was like you went through the doors and into another world where life was easy and beautiful and you remembered why you were in New York. Why all the chaos and the pain and the long days were worth it. Because places like this existed. Because people, the ones moving around with their shopping bags and maps, came from all over the world to experience this place you called home. I guess you could say the Plaza renewed my faith not just in New York, but in life, when I was feeling crushed by it.

I didn't even care about the cocktail. The bar was in another area of the hotel, a dark, plush purple area where I would order the same martini I ordered at every other cocktail bar. This wasn't about the drink or the bar. This was about that moment. That feeling. Except when we walked up the red carpeted stairs, the wind catching beneath my dress and the tails of Jay's sports jacket flying up underneath his winter coat, I felt a very different feeling as a man in the black hat and jacket put his hand up and told us the Plaza was closed for renovations.

I recognized the sensation immediately. The onrush of fury and fear. The unbelievable slamming against the believable. Reality coming out of left field and decking me. It was the same feeling that overtook me when I'd be at the airport and they'd announce that my flight was delayed. The same feeling as when a friend canceled on me last-minute after I'd been waiting all day to see them. The same fury and pain and frenzy as when I'd watch something I wanted so badly, something so close I could almost touch it, float out of my grasp. It was that childish, haunting feeling that *life wasn't fair*.

WHAT THE MOOD IS TELLING YOU

Standing on the steps of the Plaza, Jay chatting with the man in the black hat to get more information, I felt a wave of heat roll through my body. *How can this be happening? After we've come all this way? This was the only thing I wanted, a simple cocktail, and I can't even get that?* I knew it wasn't a big deal. I knew it was such a small inconvenience in the grand scheme of life, but it seemed to mean so much more. It was bigger than what was happening.

It wasn't about the drink. It wasn't even about the Plaza. It was about how nothing in my life was going right. This moment was just the tipping point on a mountain of things I felt weren't happening to me. I still hadn't sold my book. I was still working for my dad. I was still living in the same one-bedroom apartment in Brooklyn I'd been living in for the past five years. I was working so hard, had been in New York so long, and it felt like nothing was ever going to happen to me. A simple, single drink at the Plaza was just another thing I'd never have.

When Jay had finished speaking to the doorman and came to stand next to me at the bottom of the steps where I was staring out into the dead trees of Central Park, his touch opened the floodgates and the tears started pouring. He hugged me and I cried harder and louder, snot and tears staining his jacket. "Let's go get a drink somewhere else," he said, taking my hand and leading me down Fifty-Ninth Street. We walked in the cold, against the wind, my sullen steps trailing behind Jay. My body hunched over in defeat.

"Let's stop in here and figure out a new plan," he said outside a dive bar with green neon lights. Walking inside, my mood deepened. This was definitely not the Plaza. A loud, bellowing voice echoed through my left ear as I turned to see a live band. It was country music night. But there was also a game on the TV at the opposite end of the bar. A crowd of men in jerseys, yelling, high-fiving, chanting. Jay managed to find us an empty seat in between them. Pulling it out for me, he stood behind me, on his phone.

"I'm sure we can get a reservation at one of the other hotels."

"It doesn't matter," I said with a sniffle. "It's all ruined." By the time the bartender had returned with my whiskey, my self-pity had turned to rage. "Couldn't you have done some research before? All I asked was for a drink at the Plaza, that's all I wanted, and you couldn't even find out if they were open?"

There was only so much Jay could put up with, even if it was my birthday. To him, to everyone else, this was nothing more than an inconvenience in the middle of a great life. A young woman living in New York with her health and her husband who just can't get a drink where she wants. "You are a spoiled brat," he said. "A spoiled brat who can't handle anything. You think this is what I want to be doing on a Saturday night? Watching you cry over a goddamn cocktail bar?"

"It's not about the cocktail bar!" I yelled. "It's about how this always happens to me. No matter how hard I work, nothing works out."

"Life isn't fair! For any of us! Get over it!" he yelled, and stormed out of the bar, leaving me to drink two double whiskeys and contemplate exactly why this minor inconvenience felt like the end of the world. Per usual, I had overreacted. Had let a small inconvenience turn into an ordeal. Another wasted evening. Another ruined memory. But I still felt so angry. Why was this bothering me so much? What caused me to feel so personally attacked by the small events of life? It had less to do, I found out, with what the events were and everything to do with how I perceived them.

In an experiment designed to study the factors that lead

to people's disproportionate emotional reactions, scientists found four general factors that cause us to overreact: unfairness, disrespect, loss of self-esteem, and rejection. You feel:

Unfairness when someone or something causes you to think you're getting the short end of the stick. You also feel it when someone violates the social codes that you believe you're following and they're not. It's why you want to quit your job when you find out your coworker, who hasn't even been at the company as long as you, is getting that promotion you wanted.

Disrespect when you think someone or something has violated the respectful treatment you believe you're entitled to. When your husband or wife doesn't empty the dishwasher even though it's their turn. When your kids give you attitude or ask you for money after ignoring your last phone calls. When your boss asks you to do something that's beneath you. When you blow up, it's not the one thing everyone thinks it is, it's the culmination of disrespect you've been stewing on.

Loss of self-esteem when someone or something contradicts the beliefs you have about yourself. Like when you think you look great one night but no one hits on you at the bar. Or when you are expecting praise from your boss for a project but instead get a stern or disappointed email.

Rejection when someone or something makes you feel excluded. Whether it be finding out your friends all had dinner without you or you didn't get into your first choice for grad school, it's that unbearable feeling of not being chosen, invited, allowed.

This mood was all about judgment. How fair or unfair we think a situation is. Our reactions to situations are born from how we perceive the situation. In the *Journal of Personality and Social Psychology*, psychology professors Ed Diener and Randy Larsen report that differences in emotional styles are closely tied to differences in how people think about events. In their study, after asking people to keep a log of their week and all their emotional reactions, the researchers showed the participants disturbing images to gauge their level of affectedness.

A pattern emerged, with those who logged more emotional reactions throughout the week (deemed highly emotional people) focusing their attention on the worst part of the photo. These more emotional participants also had a tendency to observe events in relation to themselves, rather than objectively. For emotionally prone people, a photo of a homeless man showed not just a homeless man, but a reflection of society and how awful it is. It was a reminder of how they were living in a generation that may have no social security for them. How they could be living on the streets one day. According to Daniel Goleman, author of the *New York Times* article "Intensity of Emotion Tied to Perception and Thinking," "Those who live lives of deep emotional intensity seem to have a more complex sense of themselves and lead lives that are more complicated than do those whose emotions are less strong."

When we're sitting in traffic we don't just think we'll be twenty minutes late to work, we think about how we're probably on the boss's radar since the last time we came in late two months ago and it'll be the last straw on the ever-growing list they've secretly created about us, and we'll be called into their office and fired. It's not traffic, it's our failed career. It's not a plane delay, it's the six hours we won't be able to spend with our kids. It's not just a broken air conditioner, it's another reason we'll never be able to pay off our student loans. Anytime something happens—a delay, a stolen AmEx, a lack of response, a forgotten reservation—it's not the event that triggers us, but our judgment about it. How unfair it is. How disrespectful it is. How terrible the consequences will be.

This wasn't a death. This wasn't a sickness. This wasn't something anyone would have any pity about. I was a woman who couldn't handle life. A wife who could shroud an entire vacation in a mood for something as trivial as bad weather. If the old saying was right and "you can tell a lot about a person by the way [s]he handles these three things: a rainy holiday, lost luggage, and tangled Christmas tree lights," then what could people tell about me?

My life had been a long progression of overzealous reactions to minor, insignificant things. Every traffic delay, every missed connection, every scam felt like a personal affront. The slightest wind could push me into a mood, never mind something as serious as a lost job or flood. I didn't want to be like that anymore. I wanted to be one of those strong women. A woman who handled crises and misfortune with dignity. A woman who lost her luggage and said things like, *Oh well. They're just clothes*.

If you can manage yourself during the biggest events, you can handle yourself during any of the smaller ones. A zit on your face, an awkward family gathering; all of our moods can be seen as the inability to handle the unforeseen things life throws at us. I guess you could say that all moods start and end with how we judge their triggers. Is this that big of a pimple? Is this that bad of a family fight? Is that what he really means by that comment?

The final mood came on my twenty-ninth birthday, which coincided with the end of my journey. And the trigger was a problem that had no immediate solution. The type of problem—like a surprise visit from your mother-in-law, rain on your wedding day, or layoffs at work—that requires less fixing and more accepting. A situation I did not create, want, or ask for, but had to deal with. And I could either move through it screaming, or move through it with patience, elegance, and grace. The situation wouldn't change, only my reaction to it could.

A delayed plane is either a ruined trip or a chance for another drink at the airport. A surprise visit from your mother-in-law is either a wasted weekend or a chance to show your partner how much you really love them.

The *life isn't fair* motto has never worked for me. It didn't soothe me when things felt out of control and unjust. But if life has taught me anything it's that there's always some silver lining if you stay around long enough to find it. Life isn't fair, but there's always justice somewhere if you're willing to look for it. Because I couldn't swallow the idea that terrible things happen *just because*, I decided to look at it another way. To force myself to find an alternative meaning, and thus understanding, as to why things happened. Only when I did that was I able to practice turning the worst moments of my life into the most meaningful.

THINK OF THE FEATHERS YOU'LL GET

> In knowing how to overcome little things, a
> centimeter at a time, gradually when bigger
> things come, you're prepared.
>
> —Katherine Dunham

The Plaza story was not a good party story. Most of the small inconveniences of life weren't good enough stories to relay to my therapist, let alone a group of friends. But then a big thing happened, the kind of event that taught me how the worst things in life are like tests and if you can pass them, they become degrees you can hang on your wall.

This was three months after my birthday. It started when a woman named Gina sent me a message on LinkedIn. *I just love Words of Women,* she wrote. *I'm a lawyer at a big law firm and think I could help you if you ever wanted to expand into other things with the brand.* My interest was piqued. I replied telling her I couldn't pay her and didn't really know what there was to do, but if she had ideas, I was happy to listen.

Over coffee she seduced me. "I just think you're brilliant," she said. "I just think Words of Women could be so much more," she said again and again. Then she told me I was pretty. So, so pretty. Blushing, I told her I'd obviously love to make money from Words of Women one day, but right now it was just a passion project. An outlet for all the insights I was finding for this book. It was just my little blog. I wasn't a businesswoman and I definitely couldn't pay her. "That's okay," she said. "I'm happy with just equity."

Because she was a lawyer, she offered to draw up the papers. And because I didn't want to spend $300 to have my lawyer do it, I didn't protest. The only terms I gave her were that she could have 25 percent of Words of Women contingent on her getting funding. I figured since Words of Women was just a passion project, if Gina could find us money, she could have a percentage of it. Gina agreed and proceeded to send me lovely texts about how excited she was and all the investors she knew. Then she'd send me emails with articles about companies we could be like or be better than. I know Gina is a good lawyer because all these tactics worked. And when the contract appeared in my inbox and I was flooded by an array of ideas and promises and future plans, I was too excited, too dizzy, too distracted to read it. I just signed it and sent it back.

I wasn't going to read forty pages of a contract. Gina was so nice. Gina was my new best friend. On top of that, Gina's boyfriend got along with my boyfriend, so now I didn't just have a new friend, but we had couple friends. It all seemed perfect. Until Gina got drunk. More specifically, got drunk and told me she wanted to write a book. "I thought you wanted to help grow Words of Women?" I asked her in the dimly lit bar outside her law firm in Midtown. "I do, but I also want to write a book." She took another sip of her martini. "I think I could write a really good one about being a female lawyer. You know, surrounded by all these high-powered men." She slurred into my ear, "I know some shit."

"Oh, okay. That makes sense. Well, that's exciting." I tried to feign enthusiasm but was annoyed she was now just thinking of doing what I was doing when I needed her to do what she said she was going to do.

"Do you think I could see your book pitch?" she asked.

"Um, yeah, sure, it's not done yet, but if it helps I'll send it." I was susceptible to her charms. I also thought once she saw the fifty pages, she'd give up and move on.

Two weeks later we met up with her and her boyfriend for another drink. "I finished my book pitch," she squealed while our boyfriends huddled on the other side of the booth talking about World War II documentaries.

"Wow, so fast! That's great!" I feigned more enthusiasm.

"I really want to send it to you. Julien told me not to, but what the hell." She slurred the last word.

"Yeah, send it!" I said. But what I really wanted was to stop talking about it. How could she have finished a book pitch in two weeks? Mine took six months.

The next day at work I was bored and decided to check out Gina's book pitch. The pitch was attached to an email she'd forwarded to me. Who had she sent it to before me? I scrolled down to see the original email. It was to an agent at CAA, one of the biggest talent agencies in the world, one even I hadn't thought to pitch myself to when looking for an agent. She told them she'd written a book and was the co-owner of Words of Women. Everything went dark. It had to be a mistake. I opened the attachment and there it was, plain as day, a near exact copy of my pitch with her name on it.

I reflexively sent her an email. *Hey Gina, I just read your pitch. I have to say I'm a little taken aback by you saying you co-own Words of Women. The agreement was that you could have a percentage if you got*

*us funding. And even if you did get funding, you wouldn't be a co-owner.
I have been working on* Words of Women *for four years. I only met you
three months ago.*

Two hours later she responded: *Read the contract. I own 25% of*
Words of Women. *You signed it . . . remember?* She then had the nerve
to sign off the email with *sigh*, as if she couldn't believe she had
to explain this to me.

Snot and salt were pouring into my mouth as I emailed my
lawyer. *Can you please tell me what I signed?* My lawyer called me
back within thirty minutes to tell me the document I'd signed
wasn't a contract but an amendment to my LLC, and in doing
that I'd made her part owner of the company.

Memories of the previous nights jumped in and out. *Julien
told me not to send it to you . . . I'm happy with just equity.* My lawyer
informed me she couldn't help because this was a New York
contract, and had different rules and regulations than contracts
drawn up in California, where my lawyer practiced, and even if
I claimed I didn't know what I was signing, that would need
to be reviewed by a New York judge. A judge?! She sent me
information for her lawyer friend in New York, who informed me
her retainer was $6,000. I thanked her, told her I would think
about it, hung up, and started crying again. Foaming. Choking
on hot, salty tears. In the midst of all this, however, I experienced
one of those out-of-body moments. As I watched myself from
a distance, the words of Virginia Woolf repeated over and over
again like a mantra: "I am going to face certain things. It is going
to be a time of adventure and attack."

This was it, my moment of trial. One of those events that I
had known would eventually come, only this one wasn't death
or disease or bankruptcy, but a smaller catastrophe. This was the

first of many I'd face, and if I couldn't handle this one, I'd never handle any of the bigger ones. So I dipped into my savings, called the lawyer, and took back what was mine. It was painful and expensive and I wish it never happened, but it did and I'm happy it did because otherwise I would have never learned the lesson *Don't sign anything without reading it.*

A few weeks later, after the sting had worn off and a solution had been agreed upon, I found myself telling the story to a friend over dinner. Only this time I wasn't crying. I was exaggerating, laughing, and pausing for dramatic effect, and just two days after that my friend's friend, who heard the story through her, was emailing me to ask for my lawyer's information. She was going through a similar struggle and she wanted *my advice.* I was the one with a feather in my cap.

That expression originates from the Native Americans who would add feathers to their headdresses for every enemy slain. The larger and more robust the headdress, the more prestigious the wearer was because of it. The custom was also used by hunters; those who'd made the first kill of the hunt put the feathers in their hat to let the others know. It was an honor, a victory.

Over time, that's how experiences settle into us. They start as things we don't think we'll ever overcome. Then things we'll never get over. Then they're things we're stronger for. After more than a year, that's all Gina is to me now, a feather in my cap. Something I dealt with and came out, bloodied and bruised, on the other side of. To this day, I can honestly say it was the worst thing that happened to me in my professional life. It was the first time I had to deal with lawyers and courtrooms and the jarring realization that people will try to hurt you for their own selfish reasons. I'd been slapped across the face by reality, and hard.

Because of that, however, I had a leg up on my friends. The ones who'd eventually come face-to-face with their own moments of trial, their own scandals and real-world mistakes that could cost them real things. When it happened to them, I was that person who knew a good lawyer. I was that person with advice. I was the person who'd been there. It happened to me first, and now I could teach them about it.

Becoming a strong woman is like becoming a self-made millionaire: It doesn't happen overnight. It's years upon years of trudging and slogging and working. And when it happens, there are no trumpets or whistles. It's just something that occurs, like arthritis or wisdom, after so much time, so many *things*, so many moments, that you're not sure when you got it. You're just stronger now. You just know how to wait in line. You ask for what you want. You command rooms with order and ease. You don't flinch at awkwardness, discomfort, or the unexpected.

You're strong because you've overcome all these things before. You've waited in enough lines to know getting annoyed doesn't help. You've had enough flat tires to know AAA will eventually come (or if you're truly gifted, you'll change it yourself). You've embarrassed yourself enough to no longer care what people think. In the same way it takes ten thousand hours to master a skill, it takes ten thousand uncomfortable moments to acquire strength. And if you can look at every delay as a chance to practice patience and every breakup as a chance to strengthen your solitude, you start to see the terrible, uncomfortable, unforeseen events of life as moments to be collected and added to your arsenal of wisdom, knowledge, and personal development. Or as Jenny Holzer says, "When you start to like pain, things get interesting."

MOMENT OF APPRECIATION

> To me it is really important to live in what
> I call the spaces in-between. Bus stations,
> trains, taxis or waiting rooms in airports are
> the best places because you are open to des-
> tiny, you are open to everything and anything
> can happen.
>
> —Marina Abramović

Not every event is going to feel like a feather in your cap. Some of them will just feel like tiny, annoying things that are constantly ruining the moment. Like that time Jay and I decided to go to a movie while dogsitting for my parents back in Philadelphia. It was Friday and we were both restless from the week. It was the perfect night for a movie, one of our favorite things to do.

But this wasn't our theater. It wasn't even our town. So when the GPS said we were still ten minutes away from the theater and my ticket said the movie started in ten minutes, I started to feel that warm rush of chaotic energy sliding up from my toes. It's that energy I get when I feel like I can't control the situation. Scenarios ran through my mind, becoming more and more vivid as the minutes passed. Walking into the theater to find all the seats except the two in the front row taken was the most pressing one. I was getting upset just thinking about it. I couldn't sit like that through two hours. Why should I have to strain my neck like an ostrich?

"Can't you find a damn parking space!" I screamed.

"I don't know this area! Why do you always have to get like this?"

"I'm not getting like anything."

When we parked Jay was silent. He didn't yell. Didn't shout. Just shook his head. "I thought you were better. Clearly, nothing has changed."

"I don't have time for a lecture right now," I yelled. "Do you want to sit in the front row again?"

"This isn't New York! It won't be packed like it always is there."

"You don't know that!" I protested, two yards in front of him.

When we walked into Theater 2, my face flushed. I couldn't look at Jay. Instead, I watched him walk stoically toward the hundreds of empty seats in front of us. When we sat down, I tried to apologize in my roundabout way.

"I guess you're right. This isn't like New York."

He just grunted.

"I know you hate me."

"I don't hate you," he said. "I just don't like the way you behave. But I should know how you are by now."

"How am I?"

"Unable to deal with anything."

"I deal with things."

"No, you deal with everything like it's the end of the world."

He was right. Sitting in the empty theater I'd thought would be crowded, I felt a shift between us. I could see Jay loving me less. Even if the theater had been crowded, why did it bother me so much? *Remember when there was a time you'd have just been happy to be in a car with him? Remember when you were so excited to go on dates that it didn't matter where you sat? Why can't being together be enough?*

It was enough. I just forgot. I'd become so used to Jay, so comfortable with him, I took him for granted. I took his love for granted. But his love was the only thing I really wanted or needed. This movie wasn't important. The seats didn't matter in the grand scheme of our relationship. So why was I ruining every moment with him fretting about these small, unimportant things?

It reminded me of what my mom always said when something happened that we thought was the end of the world. *At least you have your health.* It was the first and only thing that mattered. Only when we lose our health do we realize how second-tier everything else is.

Sometimes I wonder if inconveniences happen to people for that purpose: to put life into perspective after we've shifted everything out of order. It feels like there's this invisible block we all hit when we start going too fast. This block is to keep us from going over the edge, to bring us back down to earth.

In every moment of loss there's a moment of appreciation. When we mourn the dead, we appreciate life. When we lament the state of the world, we take a moment to appreciate our neighbors. When the worst happens, we cling to the good still around. The good becomes that much more important. **You need this moment of crisis to slow you down and make you appreciate all you do have in this moment of loss.**

REALIZE YOUR PATH IS SOMEWHERE ELSE

> The best way to treat obstacles is to use them
> as stepping-stones. Laugh at them, tread on
> them, and let them lead you to something
> better.
> —Enid Blyton, *Mr. Galliano's Circus*

I was getting better at handling life's curveballs, that was for
certain. I even started to pick up a slight sense of enjoyment
from mastering, conquering, and handling things. There were,
however, still things that bothered me. These were the moments
when I felt like I was missing out on something else because of
an inconvenience. I could patiently wait in line, but I still felt
that rush of rage when someone who got in line just five seconds
before me got the last movie ticket. I could wait in traffic, but
only when there was nothing to rush home for. I was having
trouble stopping the mood when I felt I was missing something
important, when the inconvenience was getting in the way.

Then one afternoon, avoiding writing, I found myself reading about Julie Andrews. A fuzzy black-and-white video of her
from the 1964 Golden Globe Awards had been circulating and
I'd watched it three times. I was half watching because of the
genuine joy she exuded ascending the stage and half because I
didn't really understand why the video was being shared. It was

just an acceptance speech. There was nothing political. Nothing outrageous. Just a few words. After a quick search I found the true meaning behind its resurfaced virality.

To add some context, in 1963, one year before that award show, Julie Andrews auditioned for the part of Eliza Doolittle in the movie adaptation of *My Fair Lady*. Although Andrews had yet to make her transition from the stage to the screen, she'd played Eliza on Broadway for the longest run in theater history and won six Tony Awards, so this felt like her perfect break.

When Jack Warner, head of Warner Bros., bought the film rights to the show, however, he had his mind set on a different actress. So, like so many actresses, Andrews was passed over for another. This other actress was Audrey Hepburn, and even though she wouldn't be able to carry the musical aspect of the film and it would require dubbing, Warner felt the movie should have a more notable star than Andrews.

We don't know how Andrews reacted to this news. There's no written account or record that tells us if after hanging up the phone, she called her mother and cried. Or went out and got drunk at a bar. Or if she told her agent she was quitting the movie business. All we know is that, whatever she did, she didn't do it for long. Because that same year Walt Disney cast her as Mary Poppins, the lead in the film that would go on to be called Disney's masterpiece and win thirteen Academy Awards, including Best Actress.

The video that had been circulating was of Julie Andrew's 1964 acceptance speech at the Golden Globes. And the video wasn't heartwarming just because it showed a young, hardworking actress finally getting her big break, but because of how she got there. The story of her rejection, that initial drama of her being passed over for *My Fair Lady*, had circulated throughout Hollywood, so when she got onstage to make her speech, pouring out her gratitude for all those involved, there was a gasp of air, then an eruption of laughter and applause when she ended the speech by saying, "And finally, my thanks to a man who made a wonderful movie and who made all this possible in the first place: Mr. Jack Warner."

It's one of those iconic moments in Hollywood history that we love so much because it reminds us that the greatest things that happen are usually the result of something worse that happened before. If anyone knows that lesson it's actors, because if anything's more unfair than life, it's the treatment of women in Hollywood. Time and time again, they take the stage to tell the tale of how the thing that didn't happen became the thing that needed to happen. Or the thing that went horribly wrong led to the thing they did right. That's where magic happens—in the space in between what we think we want and what we get. When we're forced down a road we wouldn't be on if everything had worked out as we hoped.

The way artists can produce their best works in times of pain, life produces its best moments in times of inconvenience. And if we can open ourselves up in those moments, rather than shut down, we'll stride into that magic.

The best way I started doing this was by recording all the things that happened to me because of things that didn't. For every highlight of my life, what was the painful thing before? The thing that led me there before I realized where I was going? I created Words of Women because I couldn't get an agent or a publisher or a job. I met my husband, a good, kind man, because the man before Jay, Kevin, had a secret second girlfriend. I got that marketing job that would lead to my being able to grow and market my own brand one day because I didn't get the other five jobs I interviewed for.

When I started thinking of my life in those terms, I started seeing the delays and the lines and the unreturned calls as windows of opportunity. I wasn't getting this because something else was supposed to happen. *I am waiting on this tarmac because I need to get to Miami two hours late. Maybe it will save me from sitting in traffic and spending an extra fifty dollars on a long cab ride. Maybe it's because I'm supposed to bump into someone. I am being redirected down this road for a reason.*

Then my journal became less about the past and more about the present. I started recording all the things that were happening in the moments I hadn't planned for. What thoughts or observations did I have in the long line at CVS? What chances could I take since I had nothing to lose now that the job I wanted had rejected me? What people did I meet when I was new or alone or found myself somewhere I didn't want to be?

Waiting rooms became places of destiny. Traffic became time to reflect. Everything became this experiment of chance. I was excited for the unexpected that occurred because of the unpleasant. I started carrying my notebook around on errands, train rides, and while waiting for friends who were always late. I didn't want to forget. I wanted to be present when destiny happened. I wanted to live deliberately in the spaces in between.

REMEMBER DOWN IS PART OF UP

> But if everything was always smooth and
> perfect, you'd get too used to that, you know?
> You have to have a little bit of disorganization
> now and then. Otherwise, you'll never really
> enjoy it when things go right.
> —Sarah Dessen, *The Truth About Forever*

By the end of writing this book I was the strongest I'd ever been. After five years, I felt like I'd gone through all the moods and finally uncovered the most elusive and automatic of all of them. It was the last thread of the sweater and I couldn't wait to take the needles out before trying it on. I had what I'd always wanted: patience. I was calmer and happier and planning on moving to Philadelphia to be closer to my family. Jay and I were the best we'd been in years, and we'd just bought an apartment. An apartment that came with closing costs and unexpected fees and lots of unexpected stress, but I didn't even flinch. I was different. I was stronger. Then I looked down and noticed a hole. A snatch in the fabric. A loose thread.

It was a call from my friend Sylvia. The last time we'd spoken had been at least eight months ago, after she'd moved to France. She'd tried New York and nothing was happening. I told her I thought that was the right choice. I could see her wearing berets, sitting in cafés, and singing under a haze of smoke and blue lights. I didn't tell her that I feared for her. That what she was doing was difficult and lonely and the chances of making it felt slim.

Sylvia was my friend who nothing ever happened to. For years she'd been trying to get on Broadway, and after spending the last eight in New York she decided to move to Paris because her aunt lived there and she thought she'd have more luck in Europe. This also came after her boyfriend of ten years, the one she met in theater camp, broke up with her. Poor Sylvia. She was that one friend we all silently worried about. *When will she pack it in? When will she give up the dream? How long can this go on?*

We spoke on the phone a few months after she moved. She told me she was waitressing at a tourist trap on the Champs-Élysées. "I'm thirty-three," she said, "and still a waitress. Only now I'm a waitress in France." More months went by and though we talked less, I followed her more on social media. She was living alone in a dark studio on the outskirts of the city. I noticed bottles of wine on her empty counters. *She must be lonely*, I thought. *She'll come back soon.*

A few months later I was no longer thinking about Sylvia. My life was at a standstill and I was inhaling my own fumes. I forgot there was another side to this mood, the invisible side. The opposite of all the inconveniences and difficult moments were the nagging empty ones. The rejections. The unfulfilled dreams. The luck that never came. I knew how to stand in line and how to calmly handle leaking air conditioners, but I didn't know how to handle this part of the mood. The nagging worry that nothing would actually ever work out for me. I had gone through all the moods, I finally had everything I wanted, yet I was waking up with a feeling I'd never had before—doubt. What was next?

Why did everything feel so far away? What was there to look forward to?

Outside of the odd text here and there, we hadn't caught up in a while. The last time was when she'd texted me that she had big news. I already knew from her Instagram feed that she'd met a guy. I heard from one of my mutual friends that they were calling him the French Michael Bublé. She went on to tell me that Sylvia had been friends with a friend of his who happened to take him to her restaurant the night she was singing. They went to a party together after and now they were dating. I was happy for her. She'd been single for years, and now a guy worthy of her had come along. Over the next few months I watched her life unfold in a mirage of industry parties, weekend trips to Rome and Barcelona and Venice, nights out at Parisian restaurants we'd once stared at through wistful eyes.

Then, she called me. I was sitting at the kitchen island I always sat at, in my new apartment that was now feeling old, eating a sandwich and working on the last chapters of this book, when her name started buzzing on my screen. "Bonjour, Sylvia!" I cooed with as much fake enthusiasm I could muster. She had big news, she told me. Remember the French Michael Bublé she was dating? He'd introduced her to his agent and now she was signed. She'd be doing a demo for some French record label, a small one, but a label nonetheless. She didn't brag. It wasn't boastful. She told me all this while asking my advice. Which was that no, it wasn't too soon to move in with him, and that yes, I'd come to her album's launch party.

Only a few minutes after hanging up did I start to cry. I was happy for Sylvia, but I was miserable. I felt miserable for comparing myself to her. My life versus her life. The call just felt like another reminder of how everyone was moving on without me. How their lives were changing and mine wasn't. How I'd been working for years now and it felt like nothing was happening to me. A year ago she'd had nothing. No boyfriend. No career. No beautiful apartment in the sixth arrondissement. Now she had everything. Over the course of a day, a single moment, her life had changed.

That last thought gave me a thread of hope. Soggy ground to stand on. It only took a moment for everything to change. I let the thought sit there a little longer, marinating. I'd had plenty of moments in my life. When I met the love of my life. When I got my first break in New York. Words of Women. All of this had happened to me while Sylvia was struggling. All this had happened and yet I still felt like I was missing out.

It occurred to me that life was like this. Waves. Peaks and troughs. Highs and lows. The rhythm of life wasn't a steady line of upward momentum—we'd blaze out if it were. Instead, we get moments. Bursts of magic. Bolts of luck and change and opportunity. And then we tread again. We go back to working and striving and dreaming. And just when everything seems like it won't change, like the new dream or the new goal won't happen or the magic that came two years ago has faded and left for someone else, it comes back.

That's how it happens. You're single for years and then one day you meet someone. You think you'll never get a job again, and the one company you thought wouldn't look at you twice calls with an offer. It's long week after long week, tough break after tough break, and then the light appears. A compliment, a promotion, a breakthrough.

It's a universal rule that the moment you stop worrying and

accept where you are and what you're doing, everything changes. In the meantime, it's your duty to keep the faith. To celebrate those around you whom the magic is happening to, all while remembering that your time will come again.

If you're reading this, then you know my time eventually came. The day I got this book published was my bright moment after all the years of working without knowing, believing without understanding, and hoping without any real faith. This book in your hands is evidence that things change, just like our moods. That every bad mood can become a good one.

My time came, just like Sylvia's, and in another two, four, five years, it will come again. If it feels like everything is broken, like your life isn't going anywhere, like the threads and shards of the dream are no longer visible, remember that it's supposed to be this way. Sometime, very soon, your moment will come. Just keep up the energy to look out for it.

THE MOOD TRANSFORMED

We cannot always place responsibility outside of ourselves, on parents, nations, the world, society, race, religion. Long ago it was the gods. If we accepted a part of this responsibility we would simultaneously discover our strength.

—Anaïs Nin

Difficult times have helped me to understand better than before how infinitely rich and beautiful life is in every way and that so many things that one goes worrying about are of no importance whatsoever.

—Isak Dinesen

Every situation, properly perceived, becomes an opportunity...

—Helen Schucman, *A Course in Miracles*

ACKNOWLEDGMENTS

I've always dreamt about this part. Finally, I can redeem myself from that awful high school yearbook dedication (complete with *Sex and the City* quote). I can also set down in ink the proper gratitude I have wished to express to so many people for so long.

First, it goes without saying that this book, and my sanity, would not be here without my husband, Jarryd-Lee Mandy. In fact, Words of Women would not be what it is without his continued support, constant encouragement, and enduring patience. I owe him not just my happiness, but my success.

Thank you, Bianca Salvant, for following your instinct and introducing me to Johanna Castillo, who is the best agent a writer could ask for. Johanna, without you none of this would have been possible. Thank you for believing in me, guiding me, and occasionally talking me off the ledge. You give me the confidence, and the runway, to explore my dreams—even the more wacky ones.

Thank you to Grand Central Publishing and Hachette and all the hardworking people there who made this book a reality. Karen Kosztolnyik, thank you for believing in this project. Leah Miller, thank you for taking a chance on me and this book. Your guidance and patience enabled it to grow in ways I never imagined. And a big thank you to Maddie Caldwell, who saw me through to the end. I couldn't have asked for a more capable editor to help me over the finish line.

Then there's my good friend, Kristi Baviello, who not only read this manuscript when it was messy and without page numbers but has been my strongest advocate and cheerleader for Words of Women since we first met. Kayla Inglima, thank you for your blind support of Words of Women all these years and the many bottles of wine you have supplied. And Griffin Rauscher, who has been a great neighbor, friend, and supporter. Ladies, we will one day meet at the clubhouse again.

Of course, a big thank you to my parents. Who survived the book and the things they thought would be in it. Thank you for giving me the tools I needed to follow my dreams. And most of all, thank you for putting up with this moody child.

And finally, thank you to my Words of Women family. Over the past five years so many of you have reached out and shared your own stories, sent messages of support and encouragement, and stood by the newsletters with all its typos and missing links. You are all my family and this book is thanks to you as much as it's for you.

ABOUT THE AUTHOR

Lauren Martin is a writer and the founder of Words of Women—an online and physical community dedicated to the growth and development of women. By providing entertaining, enlightening, and supportive content related to the female condition, it has transformed the feeds and lives of its 300,000 women followers across Instagram, Facebook, and newsletter subscribers.